PROTECT YOUR IDENTITY

A Step-by-Step Guide and Workbook

CARRIE KERSKIE

Paperback ISBN 978-0-9832529-3-1

EBook ISBN: 978-0-9832529-4-8

Edited by Raven Dodd, Preserving the Author's Voice

Printed in the United States

First printing edition 2020.

www.CarrieKerskie.com

DEDICATION

I dedicate this book to the numerous victims that have entrusted my team and me with restoring their identity; and to those wanting to take back control by learning the steps to protect their identity, without having to provide a third-party with their personal information; my family and friends for your support and encouragement. I am grateful.

CONTENTS

INTRODUCTION 1

SECTION ONE: UNDERSTANDING IDENTITY THEFT 4

    MORE THAN A FINANCIAL RISK 5

    METHODS USED BY IDENTITY THIEVES 12

    YOU ARE THE BEST DEFENSE 29

SECTION TWO: THE PROTECTION PROCESS **32**

    OVERVIEW 33

    EMPLOYMENT IDENTITY THEFT 35

    SOCIAL SECURITY IDENTITY THEFT 39

    TAX RETURN IDENTITY THEFT 43

    MAIL IDENTITY THEFT 47

    NEW ACCOUNT FRAUD 50

    ACCOUNT TAKEOVER 72

    CHILD IDENTITY THEFT 79

    DECEASED PERSON IDENTITY THEFT 81

EPILOGUE: LOOKING FORWARD 83

PROTECTION PROCESS WORKBOOK 85

INDEX **99**

INTRODUCTION

I want to thank you personally for purchasing this book. You are about to begin your journey to protecting your identity. My journey began at my private investigation agency, Kerskie Group, LLC.

In 2007, we began receiving calls from identity theft victims seeking assistance. At the time, online resources were limited. The resources available were confusing. Being the type of person that doesn't like to turn away a person in need, I offered to help. The first case opened our eyes to the negative impact identity theft can have on a person's life.

Word of mouth began to spread, and we received calls from more victims. Each new case revealed complexities unobserved in prior cases. It also showed how, in some cases, if the victims had known one or two things in advance, they would not have become victims. I felt it was my civic duty to warn the residents of my hometown, Naples, Florida. I called non-profit groups offering a free presentation on the dangers of identity theft. The response received from the first group I contacted set me on a life-long path. A woman said to me, "We don't care about identity theft; it doesn't happen in Naples." I know, hard to believe. For the record, Naples, FL, would later rank in the top ten metropolitan areas for the highest number of identity theft complaints to the FTC per capita. At one time, Naples, FL, ranked third in the nation. I digress.

The moment I heard the ridiculous comment was when I knew I had found my mission: to raise awareness about the risk for identity theft. For years I presented to any group willing to listen. I even offered to refrain from mentioning the name of my private investigation agency to avoid having them think this was a sales pitch. The goal was to educate the community.

Then one day, it happened. I received a call from someone in my community that heard me speak. She said she had received a scam phone call, and if it were not for hearing me warn about similar calls, she would have given the caller her personal information—score one for the good guys. Mission accomplished!

The mission was not accomplished. Little did I know, this was only the beginning.

I started receiving requests for a book. Attendees said that there was too much information to retain from a presentation. They wanted a book. Who me? Write a book? Are they kidding? I never thought of myself as a writer. I was a C student in language arts. That was final, and I was not going to write a book.

Guess what happened, I wrote the book. In 2011 my first book, Your Public Identity: Because Nothing is Private Anymore, was released.

What made me change my mind? I visited a local bookstore to peruse the books on identity theft. I couldn't figure out what they were saying. If I couldn't understand it, and I work in this space, how was the average consumer supposed to understand it? It didn't have to be so complicated. My goal was to write a book that was easy for anyone to understand. It was about that time that self-doubt reared its ugly head. To overcome the self-doubt, I told myself that if the book helped one person, it would be worth it.

Since the release of my first book, I have received countless calls, letters, and emails from readers expressing their gratitude. The greatest compliments received were: "The information is easy to understand and use." and "Your book helped me from becoming a victim." Mission accomplished, or was it?

During the past eight years, requests for presentations, consulting, and interviews increased. Organizations were now hiring me to speak, as opposed to telling me identity theft was not a concern. While my speaking, writing, and consulting career increased, I continued to work with victims. A unique feature of my agency is that we are not a call center. When we work with a victim, we come to them. We visit them at their home, sit face-to-face. Identity theft victims are already scared and paranoid; the last thing they want to do is give all their information to a stranger on the other end of the phone or email. Restoring their identity is only part of the service. Giving them peace of mind is what matters.

When a victim contacted my agency, we would not only restore her identity; we would help to implement steps to prevent or minimize future incidents. We discovered that identity thieves often go for the easy targets. The more barriers you have in place, the harder it is to use your identity. We were making our customers less attractive to identity thieves. But did it only work for people that previously had identity theft? Could these steps be used to protect someone with no prior identity theft? Yes!

After a long couple of months of helping victims implement steps to prevent or minimize future risks, it dawned on me that other people may be interested in proactively protecting their identity. I ran the idea of writing a guide and workbook past friends and family. They agreed; a guide and workbook were needed. So began my journey of writing my second book, this book. My goal remains the same: if it helps one person, it was worth the time and effort. I hope that you agree.

After reading this book, please tell me what you think. I would love to hear from you. Send me an email at **ck@kerskie.com**. If this book helped you, tell your friends and family. You will help them protect their identity while helping me continue my mission.

SECTION ONE: UNDERSTANDING IDENTITY THEFT

MORE THAN A FINANCIAL RISK

The first step to protecting your identity is to understand the threat. Identity theft is more than a financial risk. Financial identity theft is the best known as it is the most talked about in the media. Other types of identity theft could cause you greater harm. The first step to protecting yourself from identity theft is to understand the different types and how they could impact you.

Financial Identity Theft

Financial identity theft occurs when an imposter uses your identity to apply for financial accounts.

- Bank - checking, savings, and debit cards

- Credit card

- Brokerage

- Loans

- Bankruptcy, yes, you read that right

Case Examples

A woman, in her 80's, was surprised when Federal Marshals arrived at her door with a warrant for the assets not disclosed on her bankruptcy filing. She did not file for bankruptcy. An imposter, living in another state, used her identity for years. The imposter had financial problems and, to keep up the charade, filed for bankruptcy using the woman's identity

In another case, a man discovered that $250,000 had been stolen from his bank account for over six months. An imposter used the man's identity to link the man's bank account with an American Express gift card. Each month the imposter would transfer money from the man's bank account to the gift card. The transaction was listed on the man's bank statement as American Express. The man and his family manager assumed these were his payments, which were in amounts normal for the man's American Express account. The man did not become suspicious until the imposter became greedy and took out a significant amount of money.

Utility Identity Theft

Utility identity theft occurs when an imposter uses your identity to open a utility account. Utility accounts include cable, electric, water, and phone, both mobile and landline. Bad guys will open a mobile phone account, purchase a new device on a payment plan, then sell the device for cash—all using your identity, including the payment plan.

Case Example

A victim received, in the mail, a new mobile phone. She did not order the new phone. She contacted the mobile phone carrier and discovered that an imposter used her identity to reactivate her old mobile phone number and account. Using the reactivated account, the imposter purchased the new mobile phone. The phone was delivered to the victim's residence. Not very smart.

Government Documents and Benefits Identity Theft

Government documents and benefits identity theft occurs when an imposter uses your identity.

- To apply for Social Security benefits
- To apply for Medicare or Medicaid
- To apply for Welfare benefits
- To apply for unemployment benefits
- To submit a fraudulent tax return to the IRS
- To apply for or duplicate your driver's license or passport
- To exit and enter the country, border crossing

Case Examples

A victim attempted to file his tax return using e-file. The IRS rejected the tax return as they had already received one with his identity. An imposter used the victim's name and social security number on a tax return. The imposter did not use the victim's income figures, as they were unknown. The imposter used fictitious information that would result in the largest refund with minimal risk of triggering an audit.

In another case, a woman was returning from her trip to Mexico. She was detained at the border for questioning. After three hours, she was released. The border agent told her that she was a victim of identity theft and that it needed to be corrected before she attempted to enter Mexico again. The woman reviewed her credit reports and searched for criminal records. She found no proof of identity theft. Then she contacted us. We discovered that her identity had been used for border crossing only. An imposter duplicated her documents to cross between the U.S. and Mexico. The imposter had crossed the border frequently in a short amount of time, and it triggered an alert for border agents.

A separate case involved a man that attempted to apply for Social Security benefits. He had delayed applying for benefits until the age of 70. He was surprised when the SSA notified him that he was already receiving benefits. An imposter used his identity to apply for benefits when the man turned 65. For five years, the imposter received this man's social security benefits.

Employment Identity Theft

Employment identity theft occurs when an imposter uses your identity for employment purposes. It also applies when an imposter uses your professional credentials to obtain employment.

Case Examples

A man received notification from the state's unemployment department regarding his recent application for unemployment benefits. At first, the man thought it was a scam letter. He called the state and leaned that someone had used his identity to apply for unemployment benefits. The man was retired and had not worked in over ten years.

In another case, a woman applied for a new job. The prospective employer conducted a criminal background check. The background check revealed criminal records for the woman. The woman was shocked as she had never been in trouble with the law, not even a speeding ticket. An imposter had used her identity to create a counterfeit driver's license, also known as a novelty ID. When the imposter was arrested, she presented the novelty ID containing the victim's information, resulting in the victim gaining a criminal record for crimes she did not commit.

In a separate case, a victim was contacted by the IRS for unreported income. During the audit process, they found that an imposter was using the victim's identity for employment. The imposter did not file tax returns, thus leaving the earned income as unreported under the victim's identity.

Criminal Identity Theft

Criminal identity theft occurs when an imposter presents your identity to law enforcement for a traffic citation, misdemeanor, or felony.

Case Examples

One day law enforcement showed up at a victim's home with a bench warrant for failing to appear in court. The victim was confused as he didn't do anything wrong. It was determined that an imposter had presented the victim's identity to law enforcement when he was arrested for a crime. The imposter failed to appear for a court hearing for the crime. Because the victim's identity was used, the warrant was issued for the victim. The true identity of the criminal was unknown.

In another case, a man was involved in a minor auto accident. Law enforcement arrived to take an accident report. The officer asked the man for his information. The officer ran the drivers' information in his system and discovered that the man's driver's license was suspended. The law enforcement officer asked the man if he knew of the suspension. He did not. The man had a clean driving record. An imposter using the man's identity had a horrible driving record. Except it was recorded under the victim's information, resulting in the suspension of the man's license without his knowledge.

Medical Identity Theft

Medical identity theft occurs when an imposter uses your identity to receive medical services, products, prescriptions, or insurance. Medical identity theft is the deadliest form of identity theft.

When an imposter uses your identity for medical services, the imposter's symptoms and test results end up on a medical file with your identity. If you and the imposter use the same healthcare facility, such as an ER, then both his and your symptoms and test results are entered into your medical record. When a physician makes a diagnosis, the physician reviews the information in your medical record. Misinformation in your medical record could result in misdiagnosis.

Case Example

A woman was sick and went to a store to buy a decongestant. The cold medicine she wanted to purchase was located behind the pharmacy counter. She asked the pharmacist for the medicine. The pharmacist asked her for her ID as this specific type of cold medicine was regulated. Criminals use cold medicine to manufacture street drugs.

The pharmacist told the women that she was not able to buy the cold medicine as she had purchased the allowed amount for the year. It was the first time the woman had purchased cold medicine in a few years. An imposter used the woman's identity to create a novelty ID for purposes of buying this type of cold medicine.

Business Identity Theft

Business identity theft is identity theft of a business' identity. A business identity includes the business tax ID number (the equivalent of an SSN for a person), branding, and credit history. Most of the information can be obtained online from the state's corporate registration website.

Imposters use a business' identity to

- Apply for credit accounts, such as a vendor or credit card account
- Change the organization's officers on the state's corporate records
- Create a fraudulent website to solicit business, primarily payments
- Modify the business' merchant processing account
- Use the business' merchant processing account to process fraudulent transactions paid for by stolen credit cards

Case Example

In the 1980's a man retired and closed his business. Thirty years later, he began receiving collection notices on behalf of the closed company. The victim then discovered that an imposter reactivated the corporate filing through the state and applied for new credit accounts.

WARNING SIGNS

Financial Identity Theft Warning Signs

- Unauthorized transaction on a statement

- Denial of credit

- Collections notice

- Receiving unknown credit card in the mail

- Notice from a financial institution

- Discrepancies on credit report

- New account letter or call

- Notice of frozen assets

Utilities Identity Theft Warning Signs

- Not receiving incoming calls

- No service

- Collections notice

- Duplicate transactions on a statement

- Notification of transfer of phone number

Government Documents & Benefits Warning Signs

- SS benefits not received

- SS benefits already applied for

- Explanation of Benefits (EOB) for unknown services or products

- Denied payments by Medicare

- Suspended driver's license

- Name on the terrorist watch list/no-fly list

- Notification of benefits application

Employment Identity Theft Warning Signs

- Notice of unemployment filing

- Additional income reported to IRS

- Different amount of income shown on SSA statement

Criminal Identity Theft Warning Signs

- Warrant issued or arrested for a crime you did not commit

- Suspended driver's license

- Denial of employment – criminal record found

Medical Identity Theft Warning Signs

- Insurance EOB for unknown services or products

- Denial of benefits

- Denial of insurance

- Denial of product service

- Collections notice

- Misinformation in your patient record

- Misdiagnosis

- Death

Business Identity Theft Warning Signs

- Credit report discrepancies

- Denial of credit

- Denial of vendor account or cash only

- Complaints by unknown customers

- Loss of business

- Fraudulent transactions on statements

- Notice of change on state corporate filing

- Collections notice for unknown accounts or charges

- Receiving a credit card that your company did not apply for

- Receiving a notice from your merchant processor regarding a change to your account that you did not make

METHODS USED BY IDENTITY THIEVES

Methods Used to Steal Your Identity

Identity thieves use various methods to steal your identity. This chapter contains information on a few of these methods. I want to make you aware of these methods so that you may better recognize them and defend yourself. I don't expect you to memorize every method. However, it is beneficial to become aware of them. Please note that this is not an exhaustive list.

APPS

Apps are applications designed for use on a smartphone or tablet. Many of these apps offer convenience, but they may also pose a risk to your privacy and security. After installing the app, the malware would load onto your device. It would either wreak havoc on the device or remain dormant until the device connected to a computer. Once connected, the malware would spread to the computer and do whatever it was programmed to do.

BLUETOOTH

Bluetooth technology allows two or more devices to communicate, such as a computer or a cell phone. If you do not password protect your computer or cell phone, any Bluetooth-enable hardware can connect and communicate, giving access to sensitive information.

Bluetooth does not provide a secure connection. It is best to keep Bluetooth turned off on your devices until you are ready to use it.

CALLER ID SPOOFING

Have you ever received a call, and the caller ID displayed your phone number? Or perhaps you received the fake IRS call, which displayed either the IRS or a 202-area code, the area code for Washington DC. If so, you witnessed firsthand caller ID spoofing.

Caller ID spoofing occurs when the information displayed in the caller ID is deliberately false to disguise the identity of the caller.

Unfortunately, spoofing is easier than you might think. Numerous websites offer caller ID spoofing services. Enter the phone number you wish to call, the information you want to be displayed in the caller ID, and the service makes the call via the internet. You might be asking yourself, "How is this legal?" The Truth in Calling Act, FCC rules prohibit spoofing with the intent to defraud, cause harm, or wrongly obtain anything of value. However, spoofing is permitted in cases where the person or organization has a legitimate reason for hiding their information, such as victims of domestic abuse or law enforcement agencies.

Scammers will use various tricks to get you to answer your telephone. These may include displaying:

- A local area code
- Your telephone number
- The name of a well-known organization (banks, creditors, insurance companies or the government)

DEEP AND DARK WEB

Another scenario involves a criminal buying your account information online from the dark and deep web. According to the Identity Theft Resources Center, over 900 million records have been exposed nationwide by data breaches. Keep in mind that these are only the known and reported data breaches. In my opinion, this number is much higher.

The breached information could be sold online. A name, address, date of birth, and social security number sell for approximately $1 online. If you add in credit card and bank account information, the rate increases if the credit card has an unlimited credit limit, and the fee could rise to $500. Your personal information is your greatest asset and a hot commodity. Once a criminal has the information, he merely contacts your bank or credit card company, pretends to be you, and requests the transaction. If he is unable to do it by telephone, he will use online account takeover to complete his mission.

DATA RECOVERY

What do you do with outdated technology? If you are like most people, you either donate, resell, or trash it. If you didn't wipe your information from the device before disposal, you are putting yourself at risk for identity theft.

There have been numerous cases where sensitive information was recovered from a device or a hard drive purchased online. Reformatting the hard drive is not enough. Neither is drilling a hole into the hard drive. You could put your device through a commercial shredder, and data could still be recovered. Someone would have to go through a lot of trouble and expense to get it, but it is still possible.

Think of each file, folder, etc. on a hard drive as a thumbprint. If you delete the file, it makes the space available, but the thumbprint remains. The only way to remove the thumbprint is to wipe it off. In the case of hard drive, it is wiped off by replacing the thumbprint with a series of 0's or other random information.

DUMPSTER DIVING

Garbology is a fancy word for dumpster diving. Yes, that is right, digging through the trash. Garbology has been a technique used by criminals through the ages, and still, today provides a treasure trove of information. What is in YOUR garbage? Did you throw away your credit card statement? How about your prescription bottles? Or perhaps it was that pre-approved credit card application? All of these have your sensitive information.

Garbology may very well be a violation of a county ordinance, but criminals do not care about breaking the law.

EMPLOYMENT SCAM

Today, most job vacancies are posted online. Some services claim to help you find a job. Scammers know this, and they will create fake websites or job offers to get you to send your sensitive information. Others will even contact you via phone or email with a fake job offer.

PUBLIC WI-FI

Using public (free) Wi-Fi is convenient and cost-effective, but it could end up costing you more than you know. When you use public Wi-Fi, you are sharing the Wi-Fi signal with everyone else connected to the same Wi-Fi signal. Known as a Man-in-the-Middle (MITM) attack, someone with the knowledge and skills could use the signal and observe what you are doing on the free Wi-Fi. Or the criminal could manipulate things so that you click on a link that downloads and installs malware on to your device.

The risk of using free Wi-Fi is higher today. Criminals will create a cloned version of the legitimate Wi-Fi network. The criminals will boost the signal strength of their malicious network using a device known as a pineapple. Your device, which is always looking for the strongest signal, may disconnect from the legitimate Wi-Fi network and connect to the malicious network. It is difficult to determine a malicious network from a legitimate network just by looking at the available networks. The risk of using free Wi-Fi is too great. Instead, use your cellular data plan or purchase a mobile hotspot. Yes, it is an additional expense, but one that is cheaper than having to mitigate the effects of a malicious Wi-Fi.

MALWARE

Malware is software that is created with malicious intent and installed without the owner's informed consent. Examples of malware are viruses, spyware, and trojans. Please note these are only a small representation of the types of malware.

Virus

Viruses can do more harm than shutting down your computer. Viruses can have your computer send out spear-phishing emails (see below). They can also give the creator/the criminal, complete access to your computer and everything on it, allowing a criminal to have remote access to your device and the data on it.

Spyware

Spyware is just as the name implies. It is malware that, once installed on a computer, collects bits of information over time without the owner's consent. Examples of the information collected could be websites visited, internet usage, internet buying habits, or passwords typed.

Keyloggers are a type of spyware. Keyloggers allow the criminal to monitor the actions of the computer user. It logs any keystroke, what you are typing, and more. It will record emails, passwords, web activity, etc. Keyloggers are also used by parents to monitor the internet activity of minor children. As a side note, keyloggers alone are not effective at protecting a minor on the internet. Often kids are too smart for these and can figure out how to work around them, or they will use a computer at a friend's home, the library, or on their cell phone. It is best to have an honest conversation with your kids about the dangers of the internet and let them use the computer at home. Create rules regarding what sites and procedures you do and do not approve and encourage your kids to talk openly with you when they make a mistake.

Trojan

A Trojan, also known as a Trojan horse, is malware disguised as legitimate software. An example would be when you click on a website and see a pop-up message saying your computer has a virus. The message further states that if you download the free program, it will remove the virus from your computer. If you click to download the program, you are downloading a virus onto your computer. Another technique is to offer a free download of an expensive, popular software program.

One case example involves the FBI cracking a "sextortion" case where a man, through social networking and email, could remotely install a Trojan, through a link in an email, onto the computers of teenage girls that he met on a social networking site. His actions allowed him to activate the computer's webcam without their knowledge. These girls had their computers in their bedrooms, and the criminal would activate the webcam while the girl was dressing and undressing and record the video. Then he used the images from the videos to extort pornographic images of the girls by telling them that if they did not send him nude photos, he would notify their parents. The girls gave in because they were afraid of getting into trouble because they had allowed the virus to be installed (unwittingly through the email link) onto the parent's computer.

MAN-IN-THE-MIDDLE (MITM)

MITM attack occurs when someone criminally intercepts communication between two parties to record the information without knowledge of either party. The criminal could then use that information to steal the victim's identity.

One example is where a target will attempt to visit the website of his bank; the criminal redirects the target to a website that looks the same as the bank's website. The only difference is that the website URL is not that of the bank. When the target enters his credentials, the criminal captures them.

PHISHING

Phishing emails are emails designed to look as if they are from a legitimate and trusted source. The main goal of a phishing email is to get you to do something. That something could be to either click on the link in the email or open the email attachment. Either one could result in malware, software with malicious intent, ending up on your electronic device. All of this happens without your knowledge.

Log in to verify

When you receive an email from an organization you currently do business with, such as your bank or credit card, there is a simple way to test the validity of the email. Log in to your account.

Once you have logged in to your account, you will be able to check for any messages or warnings. *Remember, do not click on the link in the email address.* You will need to go directly to the company's website by typing in the URL.

A few years ago, I received a supposed email from **Amazon.com** regarding the delivery of a recent purchase. I knew I did not order anything, but I wanted to make sure no one had hacked my Amazon account. I logged into my Amazon account and looked under order history. No recent orders were listed, so I knew the email was a scam.

An email from someone you know

If you are unable to call the person to verify it was from them, send them an email. *To do this, draft a new email.* Do not reply to the suspect email. Ask the sender if they sent you an email. If neither is an option, delete the email. If it is crucial for an organization or person to reach you, they will find another means of communication.

PRETEXTING OR SOCIAL ENGINEERING

Pretexting is a form of social engineering where someone lies to obtain your information. The goal is to get you to provide sensitive information. The pretext could be in the form of a survey or poll. One known pretext involves a call pretending to be from the fraud department of your bank asking to verify your sensitive information to remove fraudulent charges from your account.

PHYSICAL CHECKS

Some people think that writing a check is safer than making an online payment. Not true. When you write and mail a check, you run the risk of someone stealing the check. What is on the check? Your bank routing and account number. An imposter uses this information for online auto-deduction payments, creating a printable check, or providing the information for purchase online or by phone. An imposter could also use the information to transfer money out of your bank account.

PUBLIC RECORDS

Did you know that in as little as five minutes, I can find out if you own your home, how much you paid for it, if you have a mortgage, and get a diagram of your residence? Depending on the state where you reside, I and anyone else with a computer can do all of this by using online public records. Your local Clerk of Courts uploads your information to the internet. Now, some of these sites require payment, others require you to create an account, and still, others are not yet online. These are merely minor setbacks for a criminal. They can easily overcome these and get your information. I have even found older documents online displaying SSNs, dates of birth, and account information. Sensitive data is supposed to be redacted from public view. However, thanks to human error, a few may have been missed. Visit your county's website to see what information of yours available for view.

There are also data mining sites that gather the information found online and provide them to anyone that wants them for a small fee. How do they do it? They use a bot. Think of a bot as a dog that is let loose to retrieve a ball. In the case of a bot, data is the ball. The bot brings back the data to be sorted and matched by specific criteria. The entire process is automated and done in seconds. Another example of a bot is a Google search. You tell it what you want, and it retrieves the information.

In one case, a father was searching by his child's name online and came across his personal information and that of his child. It turns out a school employee mistakenly uploaded a file of all student and parent information to the internet instead of the school's intranet. The information listed everything about his child—including his name and SSN.

RANSOMWARE

Imagine getting on your computer to finish that document you were working on only to find that it is no longer accessible. Instead, you see a message demanding payment to unlock your files and folders that contain your client information or photos of your family. If this has happened to you, then you were a victim of ransomware.

Once infected with ransomware, the malware will begin to encrypt files and folders on local drives, attached drives, backup drives, and potentially any other computers attached to the same network. You will not be able to access the now encrypted files or folders. To decrypt the files and folders, you must first pay a fee, typically in bitcoins, to obtain the decryption key. Paying the fee does not always resolve the problem. There have been incidents where the hacker refused to send the decryption key even after the victim paid the requested fee.

If you suspect your device has been infected, do not attempt to open the infected files. Contact a company that specializes in mitigating ransomware. There are a few types of ransomware that contain vulnerabilities that may be overcome. Do not attempt to do this yourself. Leave it to the professionals. Visit **CarrieKerskie.com** for more information.

SEARCH ENGINE PHISHING

Searching the internet to find something has become second nature. When in doubt, Google it. But you must know that some websites were developed with the sole intent to steal your information, your money, or infect your device.

Holiday shopping is prime time for search engine phishing. Criminals know that shoppers are hoping to save money, so they will create offers too good to be true. If you were to order from one of these websites, you could be exposing your credit card information, your bank account, or your sensitive information. Employment scams such as work-from-home offers use search engine phishing.

SHOULDER SURFING

If you have ever traveled on an airplane and used your device, you may have already experienced shoulder surfing. Shoulder surfing occurs when someone near you looks at your device over your shoulder. By peering over your shoulder, the person can see what you see. Be aware of your surroundings. Avoid conducting sensitive business where someone could harvest the information that is visible to them.

Shoulder surfing could be used at an ATM or the POS terminal when using a debit card. The person in view can observe you entering your PIN as well as your credit or debit card number. The person could also use their smartphone to capture a photo of your credit or debit card. The only thing he needs to remember is your PIN.

To avoid shoulder surfing, consider using a screen cover on your device. A screen cover makes the screen only visible when looking directly at it. Side views will result in seeing a black screen. Another tip is to use your other hand to cover the keypad when entering your PIN.

SKIMMER

Skimmers are used to harvest the information stored on the magnetic stripe on the back of a credit card. They will steal your credit card or debit card information to commit fraud. Skimmers have been found in gas pumps, ATM's, and self-check-out terminals. Handheld models can be found in restaurants, or anywhere you would swipe a credit or debit card or ATM card.

The technology used to build skimmers has evolved. A new version of a skimmer, known as micro-skimmer, is virtually invisible to the naked eye. Some use Bluetooth technology to enable the criminal to retrieve the stolen information without physically retrieving the skimmer.

However, a skimmer should be the last of your worries. Federal laws protect you from liability from fraudulent transactions in a bank or credit account. Monitor your statements and report suspicious activity immediately. You typically have 30-60 days to report fraudulent transactions.

SHIMMER

You might be thinking that since you now have a chip card, you no longer need to worry about skimmers. Not true. Meet the shimmer. A shimmer, like a skimmer, harvests the information from the chip in your credit card.

SMISHING

Smishing is similar to phishing, except it uses text or SMS messaging. This message may appear to be a text message from your bank or credit card company, saying that they suspect fraudulent activity in your account. The message will include a link or phone number for you to contact the organization. If you click on the link, you run the risk of being infected with malware. If you call the phone number, you will be speaking directly with the scammers. They are very good at their job, and they are very successful in getting people to provide their information. One way is by telling the caller that to proceed, first he needs to verify his identity. Verifying an identity typically includes asking for the caller's SSN, date of birth, and other information used to commit identity theft. Or the scammer could ask the caller to provide his account number and the three or four-digit security code on the credit card for verification. Providing any of this information to a scammer would be disastrous.

SPEAR PHISHING

People often tell me they only open emails from people they know. Just because the email comes from someone you know, it does not mean that person was the sender. It could be spear phishing. Another example is when you receive a phishing email, but instead of saying, "Dear customer," it has your name.

Spear phishing emails work because they appear to come from a person you trust, such as a friend, relative, or co-worker. The purpose of spear-phishing emails either is to harvest connections, who do you know and who knows you or to install malware through links and attachments.

The best defense against spear phishing is to contact the person that supposedly sent the email and ask him if he sent it. In other words, when you receive an unsolicited email from a trusted source that contains a link or attachment, pick up the phone and call the person before clicking.

If you are unable to call the person, send them an email. *Draft a new email*, do not reply to the suspect email, and ask the person if they sent you an email. If neither is an option, delete the email. If the email were legitimate and crucial, the sender would find another way to contact you.

SURVEY/POLL

The preferred format for surveys or polls is by phone or online. Scammers tend to stay away from regular mail to avoid facing mail fraud charges. The survey topics change with the "seasons." During election season, the survey/poll refers to issues or candidates. During tax season, they refer to tax-related matters. Some are year-round such as, your favorite fast-food restaurant or your favorite place to vacation. While these may appear innocent, the answers could provide a scammer with enough information to answer security questions or figure out your password. Some survey or poll scams will start with the generic questions and then move to more invasive questions regarding your sensitive information. The scammer will state that it is necessary to verify your identity to authenticate the information. Others will ask for a "donation" at the end of the call.

Online surveys or polls are the same as the phone call, except they are distributed through email or in social media. Social media is the most common. A few examples are "What color are you?" or "Let's play a game." whereby you answer a series of questions such as name or the states where you have lived. If you look at these surveys and polls from the mind of a criminal, you can quickly see how the information could be used to gather intelligence about you.

PHYSICAL THEFT

Not all methods used are technology-based. Sometimes the good old-fashioned ways work just as well. Common locations for theft are locations where people are distracted. These include the grocery store, the beach, a concert, a bar or restaurant, or a movie theater. In these locations, a purse or wallet may be exposed or unattended while the person is distracted. Just think about the number of times have you observed a woman's purse sitting all alone in the shopping cart while she compares items to purchase or the purse that sits unattended on the back of the chair or barstool. Men will leave their wallets under their towels at the beach while they go for a swim. Concerts and movie theaters provide the perfect opportunity as they are often dark or where people cram into a tight space or get bumped into often. Once they have the wallet, they now have all the information inside of it, including credit cards, driver's license, and debit cards.

But theft is not limited to wallets. Thieves will steal laptops, smartphones, USB drives, computers, and other devices, often containing sensitive information, out of an unattended vehicle, home, or office. If these devices were not password protected, then the thief has direct access to anything and everything on it.

In-Home Workers or Service Providers

These would include, but not limited to, an A/C repairman, a housekeeper, a babysitter, or a home remodeling crew.

If you have someone in your home and your sensitive information, such as bank and credit card statements, are on the kitchen table (or anywhere else), you are putting your information at risk. With cameras on cell phones, it takes mere seconds for someone to photograph the document and go on about their business. You have no idea that your information was compromised as it is still in the same position you left it.

Also, if your supply of bank checks, or emergency credit cards, is not stored in a locked file cabinet or safe, you are putting yourself at risk. When criminals steal your checks, they do not take the next set of checks; they steal the one at the bottom or end. You do not realize the checks are missing until many months or, depending on how fast you use them, years later. The same is true for earlier statements. You have already reconciled your statement and have filed it away. If it is not locked, then the criminal will take an old statement. They don't care about what you recently charged to your credit card. They only want the credit card number and your information.

What about someone breaking into your home? Think about what sensitive information a thief would have access to if he broke into your home right this minute. All of these are reasons to make it a habit of securing your sensitive information.

Personal Computer and Wi-Fi

Your personal computer probably holds quite a bit of your personal information - information you would not want to fall into the wrong hands. If your computer(s) are not password-protected, then anyone inside of your home can access the computer, including workers previously mentioned. It only takes mere seconds to download large amounts of data onto a portable USB storage device. These devices are small enough to be concealed in a pocket, tool belt, or keychain.

Another risk is your wireless router. A wireless router is a device that allows you to work from your laptop in any room. The signal from these routers can easily reach neighbors or anyone else near your home. If the router is not encrypted (password protected), then anyone in reach can get onto your network and into your computer(s). If a criminal were to drive up and down your neighborhood looking for unencrypted networks, he would be wardriving. This technique was used to steal credit card information from many large companies. Once the criminal is in your network, he can upload a virus onto your computer and obtain your information and remotely access your computer. This same technique is used by your neighbor to steal your internet service. While your neighbor may not be accessing your information, he is still committing a crime.

TYPO-SQUATTING

Scammers are well-aware of the fact that people are prone to typographical errors. Our inability or unwillingness to proofread what we type could lead to significant harm. Not physical harm but harm to our privacy. Typosquatting occurs when someone intentionally registers the misspelling of popular web addresses with the intent to profit from typographical errors. Typosquatting is done to confuse the consumer. The confusion could be intentional or unintentional.

Typosquatting can also occur to the right of the company name. Instead of .com it may say .co, .cm or .om. The intent again is to make you think you are on the legitimate website. To better illustrate typosquatting, below are a few examples of previously known typosquatted websites.

Apple vs. Appl

Apple.com is the legitimate website to buy Apple products. However, appl.com sells fake Apple products. If you had purchased from this site, what you thought was a genuine MacBook Pro ended up being junk. The site also had a link to iTunes, but instead of registering for an iTunes account, you would have ended up registering for a service that would send SMS messages to your cellphone.

Passport application

Imagine applying for a U.S. passport online only to discover that you were on the wrong website the entire time. Many fake websites appear to be the official online passport application website. The intent is to obtain your credit card and sensitive information for identity theft or other types of fraud. Just remember that websites for government agencies end in .gov. If you are on a .com website, you should call the governmental agency to verify if that is a valid web address.

Malicious websites

Recently it was announced that the .om versions of 300 popular websites, such as Netflix and Citibank, were registered in Oman. The purpose of these websites was to install malware, software with malicious intent, onto your computer or device. The malicious typosquatted websites would redirect several times before reaching a page displaying an Adobe Flash update announcement. If the user accepted the update, the malware was installed. This malware installed was a simple adware program. Adware is advertising-supported software that displays advertisements to generate revenue for its author.

USB DEVICE

USB drives, also known as flash drives or jump drives, are small handheld devices that allow you to store numerous amounts of data, music, or videos. These are portable storage devices. These devices are small enough to fit on a key ring or concealed in a bracelet. One gigabyte (1GB) can hold over 650,000 text pages. That is a ton of information on such a small device. Downloading takes mere seconds. Install the device, click a few buttons to start downloading files, and "Bam!" in a few minutes you are done.

I am not going to explain the "few buttons" as this is not a "how to commit ID theft" book. Criminals have used this simple technique to steal customer data from businesses. Typically, it is an inside job where an employee is offered money in exchange for downloading the information.

If you use a USB device as a backup for your records, then you could also be putting yourself at risk. If stolen, and unencrypted, the information is now available to whoever possesses the unit. You have just wrapped up your sensitive files in a nice pretty bow and given it to the criminal.

Another risk is finding a USB device on the ground. What is your first instinct? Your first instinct is to pick it up and plug it in to see if you can identify the owner. What you don't know is the USB has been programmed to install software that could tell the computer to recognize it as a keyboard or install malware. Either way, your computer is exposed, and the criminal can do whatever he wishes with your computer.

VISHING

Vishing is like phishing, except instead of email, it uses the telephone or voice. Vishing can also include voicemail. Criminals have access to a tool they can use to call directly into your voicemail, bypassing the ringer. The voicemail message typically involves the impersonation of a legitimate business or uses threats, such as collection accounts, to get you to return the call. Once you call them, they begin the work to get you to reveal your sensitive information or send them money.

VOICEMAIL

Did you know that many voicemail services allow you to access your voicemail by simply calling from your phone number?

That means that someone could intentionally use caller ID spoofing to gain access to your voicemail. Your best defense is to create and use a password or PIN with your voicemail service. A password or PIN is something that a scammer would not know, greatly limiting his ability to take over your voicemail account.

WARDRIVING

Wardriving is when someone gains access to your wireless network without your permission. There is a simple solution for wardriving: password protect and encrypt your wireless router. That's it. It couldn't get any easier. If you do not know how to do it, you can hire any computer geek, or, at the very least, someone with just basic computer skills, who can help you can do it yourself. You can also call the help desk for the wireless router company.

One of the largest data security breaches in American history utilized wardriving. The criminals parked in front of a business, accessed its wireless network, then accessed its computers, uploaded a Trojan, and drove away. The Trojan gathered customer credit card information and sent the information to the criminals. It was just that easy. If someone can get on your network, they can get into your computer and your files. Your best defense is to use a strong password for your network. Do not use the one that came with your router.

Methods Used to Commit Identity Theft

There are various methods identity thieves will use to commit identity theft. As mentioned before, it is not necessary to memorize these. However, it is beneficial to become aware of these methods. Please note that this is not an exhaustive list. Methods continue to change and modify.

ACCOUNT TAKEOVER

Online account takeover occurs when a criminal has control of your account online or by phone. If you have not set up online access to your accounts (credit, bank, etc.), you have a higher chance of becoming a victim of account takeover. If you are not claiming your accounts online, you leave it open for someone else to do it on your behalf.

A criminal merely calls your financial institution, pretends to be you, provides your name, address, date of birth, and Social Security number, which he bought online for $1, and asks for online access. It is just that simple.

Now that he has control of your accounts online, he can transfer funds between the accounts, especially if your accounts are linked online. For those of you that think I am telling people how to commit a crime, think again. The criminals already know this. They hope you never find out just how easy it is, or you might take precautions to protect your accounts.

CREDIT/DEBIT CARD NUMBER

Once thieves have your credit card or debit card number, here are a couple of ways they can use the information.

CREDIT CARD BLANKS

Credit card blanks are credit cards that have not yet been imprinted or had the magnetic strip coded or attached. Thieves can buy these in bulk. Once purchased, they use a credit card stamper to imprint your information on the blank. Then they attach a magnetic strip with your information duplicating your credit card. It does not matter if the credit card blank used looks exactly like yours. The only information that matters is the imprint and the magnetic strip.

GIFT CARDS

Criminals may use a gift card as opposed to a credit card blank. Instead of imprinting the credit card blank, the criminal changes the information encoded on the magnetic strip. Criminal rings are known for buying gift cards from the Dollar Store and then changing the magnetic strip information to your credit or debit card information. Because most merchants use POS (Point of Sale) terminals where you swipe the card yourself, the cashier never looks at the card.

MOBILE PAY

To use mobile pay, all you need to do is enter your credit card or bank account information. This is an easy way for thieves to use the stolen credit or debit card information. Once it has been added to their mobile pay account, under a fake name, of course, they go shopping.

NEW ACCOUNT FRAUD

To open a new phone account, mobile or landline, you need a name, address, date of birth, and Social Security number. The company will typically run a credit report before opening the account or offering a payment plan for the mobile device.

If someone has terrible credit and is unable to get an account for a smartphone, he could use your information to get one. Or perhaps the thief does not want to pay for the new phone account. He will use your information to get one.

Another reason for someone to use your information to set up a new phone account would be to set you up for additional identity theft. Once established, the phone number is reported to the credit bureau or bureaus. This fraudulent telephone number becomes part of your personal information on your credit report or reports. It is one more piece of information from your credit report that a potential creditor will use to verify your identity.

NOVELTY ID

The driver's license is one of the most commonly used forms of identification. Thieves do not need to visit the local DMV to obtain a driver's license for your identity. All they need to do is search online for a "novelty ID." A novelty ID is a fake driver's license that has the information for one person and the photograph of another.

Novelty ID's have evolved beyond the days of kids making fake ID's to buy alcohol underage. The new novelty IDs have holograms and magnetic stripes making them nearly undetectable. Some were

so good that the only way they were confirmed to be fake was once law enforcement entered the information into their system. The photo on the novelty ID did not match the one in the state DMV database.

Some websites offer reviews of novelty IDs from various vendors. Many sellers even tell you exactly how to take and scan your photograph to make sure it looks like an official driver's license photograph. What if you don't have another person's information to use on the license? No problem. Many vendors offer to sell you the information along with the novelty ID.

Once someone has a novelty ID, he can then use it to verify the stolen identity at a bank, a doctor's office, or when getting arrested.

PHONE ACCOUNTS

Taking over your current phone account is easier than you think. The thief then calls your phone carrier, provides them with your name, address, date of birth, and Social Security number. That is all the information required to access your account. Once accessed, the thief can make changes such as setting up online access, changing your email address of record, setting up call forwarding, changing your phone (mobile), or moving your account to another carrier. If the thief has set up online access, he can make any of these changes to your account via the internet.

Why would someone want to take over your phone number? Think about it for a minute. When your bank suspects fraudulent activity in your account, the bank will call you to verify the transactions. If someone wanted to use your accounts for fraud, they would also need access to your phone number so the transactions will be authorized. If a thief is applying for a new loan or a new credit card using your identity, he knows there is a chance the creditor will call your phone number if fraud is suspected. Another reason for taking over your phone number is to bypass a credit report fraud alert.

Victims of identity theft often request to have a free fraud alert placed on their credit reports. Victims have the option of adding their phone numbers to the alert. If fraud is suspected, the creditor will call the phone number listed. If your phone number has been forwarded, then your identity thief will receive the call, not you.

PRINTABLE CHECKS

Today you no longer need to contact your bank to re-order checks. Just visit any local office supply store and pick up a few printable checks. All you need is to enter the account information on the check paper. There have been cases where the bank cleared checks with typos (e.g., Brain instead of Brian).

YOU ARE THE BEST DEFENSE

You might be tempted to take the "easy way out" and sign up for an identity theft protection service. You may be surprised to learn that the "easy way" could cause you more harm.

What Identity Protection Services Can and Cannot Do

Identity theft protection services claim to protect you from identity theft. Don't be fooled by the misnomer. Identity theft protection services CANNOT protect you from identity theft. The primary function of identity theft protection services is to monitor your credit and alert you AFTER an incident. You read that right. Identity theft protection services DO NOT protect you. They only alert you AFTER you have become a victim. Identity protection services are reactive.

No one individual or company can protect you from becoming an identity theft victim. One of the identity theft protection companies has been fined twice by the Federal Trade Commission for deceptive advertising and failure to protect customer information. What the heck are you paying for? These companies make you think that if you sign-up for their service, you will be protected from identity theft. Wrong. All that these companies do is tell you when there is a problem after it has already happened. These companies cannot and do not protect you from becoming a victim. Let's take a closer look.

Limitations of Credit Monitoring

Identity theft protection companies try to lure you by offering credit monitoring. The primary and only function of credit monitoring is to tell you there is a problem. It does not fix the problem. That would be like having your auto insurance company call you to tell you that you crashed your car after you had an accident. You know there is a problem. You need someone to fix the problem. Credit monitoring monitors your credit report or reports for any changes. Changes could include soft inquiries when your current credit card company reviews your credit report to make sure you are still a good paying client. A change could be hard inquiry, an inquiry from a company for a new loan or credit card. While these are good to know, they do nothing to fix the problem.

Another thing to consider with credit monitoring is that every credit monitoring company pulls their data from the same place, the three major credit bureaus. These are Experian, Equifax, and TransUnion. If you are interested in credit monitoring, make sure that all three bureaus are being monitored on a daily (preferred) or at a minimum, monthly basis. But what about the other credit bureaus? That's right; there are more than three credit bureaus. You will learn more about these in the New Account Fraud chapter. Currently, credit monitoring services are only for the three major credit bureaus. To monitor the others, you can request and review your free report once a year. Later in this book, I will tell you how to do this.

What if your identity theft does not involve your credit reports? Did you know that not all identity theft is credit related? That's right. If someone uses your identity to receive medical services, it is not a credit-related transaction. That means it will not trigger a credit-monitoring alert. Credit-related identity theft is only one small threat. Credit monitoring cannot detect other non-credit-related identity theft.

The Reality of "We Will Restore Your Identity"

Some identity theft protection companies claim to offer restoration services, but what you think you are getting and what you get, are not the same. You might think that when you become a victim, the company will do all the heavy lifting to repair your identity. Many do not. Most will tell you what to do, and then you do all the work yourself. Or even worse, they mail you a do-it-yourself repair kit. What they don't do is explain your rights to you or tell you the questions to ask so that your identity can be restored effectively and efficiently. Restoring your identity is new to you. You have never been a victim before. How are you expected to know what to say to the companies even if you have a list of general tasks to complete? The average victim spends 200-300 hours trying to restore his identity. I know this to be true as many of the identity theft victims I have worked with have spent, on average, three months attempting to restore their identity themselves. So why are you paying for an identity theft protection service?

Beware of Creative Marketing

One of my favorite marketing gimmicks used by identity theft protection services is their claim to scan the dark web. They claim to scan the dark web to determine if your information is available for sale. It is impossible to scan or monitor the entire dark web. There are a few websites you could use to determine if your information was exposed in a data breach.

One of these websites is **https://haveibeenpwned.com/**. Besides, there is a good chance your information was compromised and sold online. Since 2005 over 1.6 billion personal records were exposed in data breaches. My information was exposed in a 2008 health care data breach. When it comes to identity theft protection services, don't fall for creative marketing. There is a better alternative.

You Can Do It Yourself

As previously mentioned, no one individual or company can protect you from becoming an identity theft victim. While preventing all identity theft is impossible, there are steps you can take to avoid or minimize/reduce your risk of specific types of identity theft. I am an expert on identity theft, yet I cannot prevent someone from using my social security number to apply for a job. I can, however, put barriers in place to make it difficult for someone to use my information. The goal is to make your identity so difficult to use that the criminal moves on to an easier target. Becoming a difficult target is easier than you think. All you need to do is to implement the steps outlined in this book.

Nobody knows you better than you. Yes, financial institutions may alert you to suspicious activity in your account. However, they cannot detect all fraud. The only way for them to do it 100% effectively would be to ask you to verify every single transaction. You would become annoyed and move to another financial institution. You know what is normal for you. You know what is NOT normal for you. You are the best equipped to detect fraudulent transactions. Just look for the warning signs discussed in the previous chapter.

Another benefit of doing it yourself is that you do not have to provide your sensitive information to a third-party. When you use an identity theft protection service, you are asked to provide the company with your SSN, bank account, and credit card information. The more you want them to monitor, the more sensitive information you will have to provide. One more company that you hope will not suffer a data breach, exposing your information. Don't fool yourself by thinking, "They won't have a breach." Remember Equifax? In September of 2017, Equifax announced a data breach that exposed the information of 147 million people. Many of these people were unaware that Equifax had their sensitive information. So, why would you willingly give your sensitive information to another company? Do it yourself.

SECTION TWO: THE PROTECTION PROCESS

OVERVIEW

Before diving into the steps of the protection process, I want to provide you with an overview and a few tips.

This section outlines each step of the prevention process. You are not required to do every step. You choose which steps you want to implement. The more measures you implement, the less attractive your identity will become to identity thieves.

The best way to use this book is to read through each chapter of this section before taking action. Each chapter explains the reasoning behind each step, enabling you to make an informed decision. After each chapter, you'll find step-by-step instructions and a worksheet to record your progress. Remember, read through the entire book before deciding which steps to implement.

When my company implements these steps for our clients, the process takes between three to four hours. You do not have to implement all the steps at the same time. This book was written to enable you to implement the steps at your convenience.

Important to Know

These steps should be completed at home on a secure internet connection and where you have access to your financial records. The organizations referenced will ask you identity verifying information based on your credit history. Refer to your financial records and printed credit reports to help you answer the questions.

At the end of each chapter is a worksheet to record your progress. For example, when placing a credit freeze, you are assigned a PIN. The PIN is used to lift or remove the freeze. You can record the PIN for each credit bureau (they will be different) in the corresponding worksheet at the end of each section. You will need to refer to the information entered in the worksheets from time to time, so keep it handy.

IMPORTANT: The information recorded in the worksheets is PRIVATE and must be protected. Secure it in a locked file cabinet or hide it. Just remember where you hid it. I have hidden things so well that I cannot find them.

Towards the end of this book is the entire workbook, comprised of the worksheets. You can use these for a spouse, or you can record all your progress in the workbook as opposed to the end of the chapter. Another option is to use the downloadable PDF version available at my website **CarrieKerskie.com/ProtectYourIdentity**. While there, you can join my newsletter.

A Note About Links and Contact Information

The links, phone numbers, and instructions were accurate as of the date of publication. The organizations referenced could change their web links, contact information, instructions at any time. It is unreasonable to hold me accountable for such information as it is out of my control. Depending on when you purchased this book, if a link, phone number, or other information no longer works, contact the company referenced at their website or by phone.

EMPLOYMENT IDENTITY THEFT

Employment identity theft is one of the most difficult types of identity theft to monitor. Credit reports may show some employment information, but not all.

How Does it Occur

Buying an identity, complete or synthetic, is easier than you might think. Synthetic identity occurs when your SSN is used with a different name and date of birth. Due to the numerous reported data breaches, sensitive information is readily available if you know where to get it. The Identity Theft Resource Center's website reveals that since 2005 nearly 1.6 BILLION records have been exposed through data breaches nationwide. And these figures are based only on known, reported data breaches.

Enter E-Verify

E-Verify, previously known as The Basic Pilot, was established by the Illegal Immigration Reform and Immigrant Responsibilities Act of 1996 (IIRIRA). The program was created to provide an internet-based program to help employers verify the employment eligibility of potential employees, both US citizens and noncitizens.

The information provided by the mandatory I-9 form is used to verify the applicant's employment eligibility. The I-9 asks for basic information such as social security number, date of birth, address, other names used, and citizenship status. The form also requires that the applicant provide two forms of ID such as a driver's license or passport and a social security card.

View the full form including the list of eligible documents at
https://www.uscis.gov/sites/default/files/files/form/i-9.pdf

The usage of E-Verify by an employer is voluntary. It is also used by some federal contractors or those mandated by state law. To see a list of states where usage of E-Verify is mandatory, visit http://www.ncsl.org/research/immigration/state-e-verify-action.aspx

Currently, over 600,000 employers nationwide use E-Verify.

E-Verify and Identity Theft

NOTE: this is the most time-consuming step and may not be necessary for everyone. You may wish to skip this step and return to it at a later time.

E-Verify is an effective tool against employment identity theft for four reasons.

1. Detects synthetic identity theft
2. May detect complete identity theft
3. Permits you to view previous inquiries
4. Provides "Self-Lock"

E-Verify Options

- SelfCheck enables anyone over the age of 16 to verify their employment eligibility.
- MyE-Verify is an online account you can create to view reports and lock your E-Verify information.
- SelfLock allows you to protect your information by placing a "lock" on your social security number. The lock expires after one year and can be unlocked at any time by logging in to your MyE-Verify account.
- Case History is a historical report of all E-Verify inquiries using your social security number.

To learn more or to create your MyE-Verify account, visit **https://www.uscis.gov/e-verify**.

Get Started

- Visit **https://myeverify.uscis.gov/**
- Agree to the terms
- Click on "Create Account"
- Follow the instructions to create your account
- Once your account has been created select "Self Lock"

- Follow the instructions to complete the process
- Amount of time to complete is 10-30 minutes
- Anyone over the age of 16 can use E-Verify self-check and lock

EMPLOYMENT IDENTITY THEFT WORKSHEET

My E-Verify

To learn more about E-Verify visit **https://www.e-verify.gov/**

To create a My E-Verify account visit **https://myeverify.uscis.gov/**

Created My E-Verify account on _____(date)

Username

_____

Password

_____

Backup Code

_____

Password Reset Questions

Question One

_____

Answer

_____

Question Two

_____

Answer

_____

Question Three

_____

Answer

_____

Question Four

_____

Answer

_____

Question Five

_____

Answer

_____

EMPLOYMENT IDENTITY THEFT WORKSHEET

Self Check

Checked on _____(date)

NOTES:

Self Lock

SSN Locked on _____

Expires on _____(one year)

Challenge Questions

Question One

_____

Answer

_____

Question Two

_____

Answer

_____

Question Three

_____

Answer

_____

To learn more about self-lock visit **https://www.uscis.gov/mye-verify/self-lock**

NOTES:

SOCIAL SECURITY IDENTITY THEFT

In January of 2013, the Social Security Administration launched a new program allowing anyone over the age of 18 to set up and manage their benefits through the online account called MySSA, My Social Security Account. The purpose was to allow consumers to apply for or manage their benefits online. Unfortunately, most consumers were unaware of this new feature. However, there was a group that was very aware of this new program—identity thieves.

Since the launch of the program, every case of social security fraud I have investigated, I traced back to MySSA as the source. Your initial thought might be that the program had a data breach or was hacked. Nope. The problem was that the victims did not set up their MySSA account; an identity thief did it on their behalf. Once established, the thief could change where the benefits are direct deposited, or he could apply for benefits before the victim applied for them. The fact that the victims had not set up their online MySSA account caused them to become victims.

Options Available

To prevent someone from setting up your MySSA account, you have two options.

1. Set up your online account.
2. Tell the SSA that you want to opt-out of electronic access

Setting Up Your Online Account

Only one account is permitted per social security number. By setting up your MySSA account, you are preventing someone else from doing it on your behalf.

To create your account, visit **www.SSA.gov** and click on the box, "My Social Security." You will be required to enter your name, address, date of birth, and social security number. Note: the site uses the latest security measures to protect your information. Next, you will be asked a series of questions based on the data on your Equifax credit report. Questions asked could include

- How much is your mortgage payment?
- What is the address of the property where you have the mortgage?
- How much is your car loan payment?

A new feature is two-factor-authentication. You will be asked to provide a cell phone number. Any time you log into your account, you will receive a text message with an eight-digit code. You will enter this code along with your username and password to log in to your MySSA account.

If you have a credit freeze on your Equifax credit report, you may need to temporarily lift the freeze before setting up your MySSA account online because the SSA uses the information on your Equifax credit report to attempt to authenticate your identity. If you have a credit freeze, the SSA might not be able to view the credit report and authenticate your identity. Recently, a few of my clients were able to successfully open their MySSA even with a freeze on their Equifax credit report. You will learn more about a credit freeze shortly.

Opting-Out of Electronic Access

For those of you that prefer to avoid online access, you have the option of opting-out of electronic access blocking you or a thief from setting up a MySSA account under your social security number. However, it is essential to know that if you choose to opt-out of electronic access, you will no longer be able to use the automated telephone services. Any changes to your account will require you to speak to a human either in-person or by telephone.

If you are looking for ways to reduce your risk of identity theft, establishing your MySSA account is one more layer of protection available. Best of all, it is free. Remember, this is available to anyone over the age of eighteen.

Employment Identity Theft Monitoring

You might be thinking that a MySSA account is only for individuals receiving benefits. Not true. By establishing your MySSA account, you will be able to view your reported-income-summary statement online. The reported income listed on the statement is provided to the SSA by the IRS. This report could be used to monitor employment identity theft. The employer is required to report the earned income to the IRS under your social security number. The report reflects income reported to the IRS under your SSN. When you review your report, if the reported income listed is more than you reported on your tax return, it could be a red flag for employment identity theft.

Right now, this is the only way to monitor employment identity theft. Keep in mind that a discrepancy in reported income does not always mean employment identity theft. Reporting errors have been known to occur. Report the discrepancy to the SSA, and they will verify the information with the IRS.

Get Started

- Visit **https://www.ssa.gov/**
- Click on "My Social Security"
- Click on "Create Account"
- On the sign-in page click on "Create Account" or "Block Electronic Access"
- Follow the steps to complete the process
- Remember, anyone over the age of 18 can create a MySSA
- Every year SSA will require you to create a new password. You will receive the reminder via email
- Approximate amount of time complete is 30 minutes

SOCIAL SECURITY IDENTITY THEFT WORKSHEET

MySSA

*Visit **www.ssa.gov** to create an account or block electronic access*

(check one) Created account_____ Blocked access_____

Created on _____(date)

Username _____

Password _____

Security Questions

Question One_____

Answer _____

Question Two_____

Answer _____

Enhanced security: _____Text _____Email _____Other

NOTES:

TAX RETURN IDENTITY THEFT

The Problem

Tax return identity theft occurs when someone files a fraudulent tax return using your personal information. In recent years, imposters started filing a fraudulent tax return using the identities of college-age students. The purpose is to obtain a refund. Then when you submit a tax return, you are told the IRS already received one for you. If you were expecting a refund, expect a delay while the IRS tries to determine which one is the correct return.

How They Do It

The only information belonging to you on the fraudulent tax return is your name and SSN. The amount of income and deductibles are numbers created by the imposter to give him the most substantial refund without triggering an audit. It does not matter if you had previously received a refund or if you had to pay taxes. The IRS does not verify the figures on a filed return before processing the refund.

The Solution

To combat tax return identity theft, the IRS launched an Identity protection (IP) PIN program. An IP PIN is a six-digit number provided to you by the IRS. You will enter the IP PIN on your tax return in the space provided. Failure to write your IP PIN on your tax return could result in the IRS rejecting your tax return. Every year the IRS provides you with a new IP PIN for the corresponding year's tax season. An IP PIN is your greatest defense against IRS tax return identity theft.

Note: an IP PIN is not the same as the PIN that you might use to track the status of an electronically filed return.

Who Can Request an IP (Identity Protection) PIN

You can choose to participate in the IP PIN program if

- You received an IRS letter inviting you to "opt-in" to get an IP PIN, **or**
- You filed your federal tax return last year with an address in Florida, Georgia, District of Columbia, Michigan, California, Maryland, Nevada, Delaware, Illinois, or Rhode Island.

How To Request an IP PIN

1. Visit **https://www.irs.gov/Individuals/Get-An-Identity-Protection-PIN,** or you can go to the IRS website **www.IRS.gov** and enter "IP PIN" in the search box located in the top right corner of the IRS home page. Please note that for those that are "married filing joint" status, only the primary filer can obtain the IP PIN.

2. Once on the "Get an IP PIN" page, read the instructions and click on the "Get an IP PIN" button located in the "Step 3" box.

3. If this is your first time using the IRS website, you will need to create an account, a UserID. To lift or remove the freeze temporarily is highly beneficial if, for some reason, you misplace your IP PIN. If you have used the "Get a Transcript" or "Online Payment Agreement," you can log in using your previously created UserID.

4. After establishing your UserID account, you can then begin the process to request your IP PIN. This process includes asking you for your name, address, date of birth, social security number as well as identity verifying questions based upon the data from your Equifax credit report.

5. If you were able to answer all questions correctly, your IP PIN would be displayed. PRINT THIS PAGE. Make sure you provide your tax preparer with a copy of your IP PIN.

For those of you that are "married filing joint" status, if both of you have IP PINs, the tax form has an "Identity Protection PIN" space for each of you to enter your IP PIN. Therefore, if both spouses have their IP PINs, then you must enter each spouse's IP PIN separately on the return, or the IRS could reject the return.

In the event your spouse previously received an IP PIN due to tax return fraud and you, the primary filer, do not have an IP PIN, then you would leave the "Identity Protection PIN" space empty. Your spouse would enter her IP PIN in the "Identity Protection PIN" to the right of her signature and occupation.

In early January, the IRS mails IP PIN notifications. Once received, store it in a secured location until it is needed to file your tax return. If you use a CPA, give a copy of the notification to your CPA.

As I have stated before, identity theft is not preventable. But there are steps you can take to reduce or eliminate specific types of identity theft. For tax return identity theft, your best defense is an IP PIN.

Get Started

- Visit **www.IRS.gov**
- Create an online account with the IRS.
- Determine if you are eligible to apply for an IP PIN
    - You received an IRS letter inviting you to "opt-in" to get an IP PIN,
    - You filed your federal tax return last year with an address in Florida, Georgia, District of Columbia, Michigan, California, Maryland, Nevada, Delaware, Illinois, or Rhode Island.
- If eligible, apply for an IP PIN by visiting Visit **https://www.irs.gov/Individuals/Get-An-Identity-Protection-PIN**

TAX RETURN IDENTITY THEFT WORKSHEET

IRS Online Account

Created IRS online account on _____(date)

Username

_____

Password

_____

Site Phrase

_____

Site Image Description

_____

IRS IP PIN

To learn more about the IRS IP PIN and to request an IP PIN visit

https://www.irs.gov/identity-theft-fraud-scams/get-an-identity-protection-pin

Requested IP PIN on _____(date)

PIN _____ Tax Season _____

NOTES:

MAIL IDENTITY THEFT

Mail theft has existed for years. Before the digital age, thieves would physically steal your mail out of your mailbox. Now, thanks to technology, thieves can walk into any United States Postal Service location, complete a change of address card, and turn it in. Soon, your mail will be sent to a new address. It is that easy.

The USPS has implemented a few steps to deter fraud, but they are not as effective as they had intended. If asked for proof of ID, the thief could present what is known as a novelty ID, or a counterfeit ID. A quick internet search reveals numerous websites selling novelty IDs. Many have the latest anti-fraud features, such as hologram and UV ink.

The USPS started mailing a change of address notification letter to the old address and the new address. The goal was to make you aware of the change. Unfortunately, the letter could take weeks or more to arrive at your old address.

Their latest feature to prevent mail theft appears to be the most effective. The service I am referring to is the Informed Delivery service. The USPS scans each piece of mail. The scanned images are stored. When you register for Informed Delivery, the USPS will send you an email every morning with images of what will be delivered to your mailbox that day. Here is the explanation of Informed Delivery from the **USPS.com** website

"Informed Delivery allows you to view greyscale images of the exterior, address side of letter-sized mailpieces and track packages in one convenient location." *

I am the type of person that likes to test things and take them apart. I want to understand how they work and, if needed, how to repair them. During my test of Informed Delivery, the email reflected five pieces of mail scheduled for delivery. I only received four pieces of mail. The missing mail was delivered the next day. I mention this, so you do not panic if a mailpiece does not arrive on the exact day. Give it another day. If you have not received the missing mail after a couple of days, contact the USPS.

Informed Delivery is a great way to monitor for physical mail theft. But, what about mail forwarded with the change of address card?

My company offers service to defend against identity theft, fraud, and cyber threats for individuals and families. One of our customers originally came to us with a complex case of identity theft, including the compromise of the person's email. Until his email account was secured, our customer asked us to manage his alerts, including Informed Delivery. Months after registering him for Informed Delivery, we received an email notification from the USPS. Someone had submitted a change of address request on behalf of our customer. The email notified us of the suspension of his Informed Delivery service until the change of address request was verified. The USPS mailed a letter to the old and the new address. In the letter was a code to confirm the request. Because our customer had an online account with the USPS, he would log in and provide the code found in the letter. The imposter, not having an online account, was unable to do the same. After our customer entered the code online, the USPS canceled the fraudulent change of address request. My customer began receiving his mail at the correct address. The process took approximately ten days. During which time, the USPS held his mail.

To activate Informed Delivery, you must first create an online account with the USPS. Online accounts are by person, not address. If two people live at the same address, each person must create their own USPS online account and activate Informed Delivery. If not, a thief could redirect a person's mail undetected.

One of our identity theft victims had her mail forwarded to another address. She was unaware of the change for almost two months. She was still receiving mail. However, she received mail addressed to her husband or her and her husband. Mail addressed to her only, was diverted to the thief. If she and her husband had registered for USPS online accounts and activated Informed Delivery, she would have been aware of the change BEFORE the thief received her mail.

Get Started

- Visit **https://www.usps.com/**
- Click on "Register" on the right side of the top menu

- Click on "Sign Up Now"
- Follow the instructions to create your account
- After your account has been created click on "Preferences" from your profile
- Select "Informed Delivery" (personal accounts only, no business)
- Follow the instructions to complete the process
- The approximate amount of time to complete is 30 minutes
- One person per account, an address can have more than one account

MAIL IDENTITY THEFT WORKSHEET

United States Postal Service

Visit **https://www.usps.com/** to create your online account

Online Account

Created on _____(date)

Username

_____

Password

_____

Security Questions

Question One

_____

Answer

_____

Question Two

_____

Answer

_____

Informed delivery activated ____Yes ____ No

Activated on _____(date)

NOTES:

NEW ACCOUNT FRAUD

New account fraud occurs when an imposter opens a new credit account using your identity. Credit accounts include loans, credit cards, and utilities, such as cellular telephone accounts.

How Do They Do It?

As previously mentioned in this book, imposters can purchase your personally identifying information, such as name, date of birth, and social security number, online for approximately one dollar. The imposter uses this information to apply for credit accounts online. Most financial institutions and credit card companies accept new credit applications on their websites, making it very convenient for imposters to commit new account fraud.

After a creditor receives an application for a new credit account, the creditor will obtain a copy of the applicant's credit report. In the case of new account fraud, your information is on the application; your credit report is received and reviewed by the new creditor. If approved, the new credit account will be opened. Remember, you did not apply for the new credit account; it was an imposter that fraudulently applied for the new credit account.

The Solution

You have three options to protect yourself from new account fraud.

- Fraud alert
- Credit freeze
- Credit lock

Fraud Alert

A fraud alert is a disclaimer added to your credit report. There are no fees associated with a fraud alert. It is free. Here are a few examples of a fraud alert disclaimer

- This person is a victim of identity theft. Please verify the consumer's identity before opening a new account.

- The consumer has requested a fraud alert. Contact the consumer at xxx-xxx-xxxx before opening a new credit account.

A fraud alert expires after one year. If you are a documented victim of identity theft or active military, you can request, in writing, for a seven-year extension on your fraud alert. Upon expiration, the credit bureau removes it from your credit report.

To create a fraud alert, contact one of the credit bureaus, and that credit bureau will notify the other two on your behalf. It only applies to TransUnion, Experian, and Equifax. To place a fraud alert with Innovis and NCTUE, you must contact them directly. You will learn more about the credit reporting agencies in the next lesson.

A fraud alert was designed to serve as a warning to a potential new creditor to minimize the risk of new account fraud. However, creditors are not mandated by law to abide by the fraud alert. It is merely a suggestion. We have observed individuals that became victims of new account fraud while their fraud alert was active.

Credit Freeze

A credit freeze prohibits the credit reporting agencies from disclosing your credit report to new creditors. If a creditor cannot review the credit report, the creditor cannot determine if the applicant is eligible for the new account. Therefore, the new account will not be opened. A credit freeze is your best defense against new account fraud.

A credit freeze does not have any impact on your current credit accounts, such as an equity line of credit or a credit card. It only applies to new lines of credit or requests for an increase in a credit limit.

A credit freeze is free for life due to an amendment to the FCRA in September of 2018. Establishing a credit freeze is free. Temporarily lifting a credit freeze, when you need to permit a new creditor to review your report, is free. Removing a credit freeze is free. A credit freeze, once established, is permanent until you either temporarily lift it or permanently remove it.

To establish a credit freeze, you must contact each of the credit reporting agencies directly. Once established, you will receive a PIN from each credit reporting agency. The PIN is what you will use to lift or remove the freeze. People often confuse a fraud alert and a credit freeze. The following chart further explains the difference between a fraud alert and a credit freeze.

FRAUD ALERT VS CREDIT FREEZE

FRAUD ALERT	CREDIT FREEZE
• Call one bureau to establish with all three	• Contact each bureau directly
• No PIN	• Requires a PIN to lift or remove
• Expires	• Remains until you lift or remove
• Free	• Free to activate, lift, and remove
• New creditors **can** view the credit report	• New creditors **cannot** view the credit report
• Limited protection from new account fraud	• Better protection against new account fraud

Credit Lock

A credit lock is similar to a credit freeze and also prohibits a credit reporting agency from disclosing your credit report to a new creditor. However, with a credit freeze, your rights and associated fees are mandated by federal law. A credit lock is a contractual agreement between you and the credit reporting agency. You must read the contract to confirm that you are not limiting your rights afforded to you by federal law. Unlike a credit freeze, the credit bureaus could charge a fee for a credit lock. A credit freeze is free for life, as mandated by the FCRA.

The credit reporting agencies do not want you to have a credit freeze as you are interfering with their business model. CRAs earn revenue by selling your credit report. A credit freeze prohibits them from selling your report. CRAs cannot prevent you from establishing a credit freeze, so they offer you a credit lock. They have developed marketing campaigns to demonstrate how convenient it is to have a credit lock and that a credit freeze is too time-consuming and difficult to manage. Not true. I have a credit freeze and can tell you that it took me less than ten minutes to temporarily lift my credit freeze before applying for new credit. Don't believe their creative marketing. Get a credit freeze. You will thank me later.

More Than Five Credit Reporting Agencies

You may be familiar with the three major credit reporting agencies (CRAs).

- Experian
- TransUnion
- Equifax

However, there are two more you need to know about to protect yourself from new account fraud.

- Innovis
- National Consumer Telecom and Utilities Exchange

Innovis is a newer CRA. However, their database is becoming more robust. We are beginning to see more creditors requesting credit reports from Innovis. The National Consumer Telecom and Utilities Exchange (NCTUE) is used primarily by the utility industry. We have observed that more mobile telephone carriers and cable companies are reporting to and requesting credit history reports from the NCTUE. Because both of these are relatively new, they may or may not have a report on you. The only way to find out is to request your credit report from each of them.

Equifax, Experian, TransUnion, Innovis, and NCTUE are only five of many CRAs. To learn more about CRAs and how you can request your consumer report from each one, download the report from the Consumer Financial Protection Bureau (CFPB) website.

Review your credit reports

Before you begin...get your credit reports; the reports can be used as a reference to aid you in setting up your online accounts. Many of the organizations referenced in the protection process workbook require validation of your identity. One of the methods used is to ask you knowledge-based questions based on the information in your credit history. You must answer the questions correctly to validate your identity.

Be Aware of Free Credit Reports Online

Advertisements for free credit reports are on television, radio, and online, but are they truly free?

What is permitted by law?

First, let's examine the law regarding access to credit history reports. The Fair and Accurate Credit Transaction Act, FACTA, states that you are entitled to receive one free credit report from each Credit Reporting Agency, CRA, every twelve months. To get your free credit reports, you can contact each credit bureau by phone, by mail, or online. You can also visit **www.AnnualCreditReport.com,** where you can request your free credit reports from all three of the major credit reporting agencies: Equifax, TransUnion, and Experian. AnnualCreditReport.com was developed by the Federal Trade Commission and the three major credit reporting agencies to make it easier for you to access your free reports.

So why are there so many websites offering free credit reports?

Plain and simple, it is a marketing gimmick. The purpose of offering free credit reports is to get you to provide information in exchange for the free credit report. That information can then be used, sold, or shared with the website's partners or, in the case of illegitimate websites, to be sold online to identity thieves.

Illegitimate (Scam) Websites

The sole intention of illegitimate websites offering free credit reports is to obtain sensitive information. It is becoming more and more difficult to determine which websites are legitimate and which are not. The scam websites look like legitimate websites. The website may have https and a padlock, which we are often told to look for before entering sensitive information online. Bad guys can pay for https to get the locked padlock. Illegitimate websites could show up in the results of an online search for free credit reports. Just because a website is listed does not mean that it is a safe website. Because of this is, it is best to avoid searching online for "free credit reports." Stick to well-known websites such as credit reporting agencies (Equifax, Experian, and TransUnion) or **AnnualCreditReport.com.**

Bait-n-Switch Websites

These websites offer you access to your credit reports for free. However, before you can view your credit reports, you must register and pay for credit monitoring. There are two problems with these websites.

1. The credit reports you receive are not the full credit reports. You will receive a summary report that contains information from all three credit reporting agencies. However, the summary report does not contain all the information from your credit history reports. Why not request your credit history report from **AnnualCreditReport.com** and receive all the information?

2. The website may offer you a free trial of their credit monitoring but then require you to enter a credit card number. Some of these websites will immediately charge your credit card for the monitoring service or make it nearly impossible to cancel the service. To make matters worse, these types of charges are often difficult to dispute with your credit card company as you have entered into an agreement with the company and have authorized the transaction or transactions.

Legitimate Websites with Creative Marketing

Then there are the websites that use "free credit report" to entice you to use their service. A red flag of these types of websites is that their services are provided free of charge. Companies cannot survive without generating revenue. If they are not generating revenue from you, ask yourself, how are they generating revenue? Is it from selling your information or through ad placements? Many of these free services are merely an advertising agency disguised as a free service. Here is a closer look at the terms of service agreement for a popular website promoting access to free credit reports and scores. I have replaced the name of the website with "company."

1. They provide you with free credit reports from two major credit bureaus. You must review all credit reports because not all creditors report to all three credit bureaus. Evidence of identity theft could be on the third report not provided to you from "company."

2. You are giving them consent to obtain your credit information at any time.

   *I understand that I am providing written instructions in accordance with the Fair Credit Reporting Act and other applicable law for "company" and affiliated companies to request and receive copies of consumer reports, scores and other information about me from third parties, including, but not limited to, TransUnion and Equifax. **I understand that my instructions let "company" and affiliated companies obtain such information at any time for as long as I have a registered "company" account to use as described in the Terms of Service and Privacy Policy.***

The privacy policy for the same website reveals additional information.

1. *What information we collect.*
    Personal Information: *This is information that identifies you personally, such as your full name, street address, email address, Social Security number, or phone number.*
    Non-Personal Information: *This is information about you or your household that doesn't identify you personally, like your gender, income, or what types of financial products you're interested in.*

2. *When we share the information we collect.*
    We do NOT *share your credit reports or scores with unaffiliated third parties (except agents acting on our behalf; we explain that below).* Translation: they share your information with affiliated third parties.

3. *Canceling your membership and deactivating your account.*
    Due to our recordkeeping and information retention requirements, ***we do not delete information about you upon deactivation.*** *We will, however, disable your account and stop sending you further communications.* Translation: they keep your information, but they will stop sending you ads and other promotional emails.

As you can see, when you use these types of web services, you may be providing your information to multiple organizations or permitting the organization to retain your information even after you have terminated your account.

Where to get your free credit reports

Federal law permits you to receive one free credit report every twelve months from each credit bureau. There is **ONLY ONE** website to use, **AnnualCreditReport.com.** The website was created by the Federal Trade Commission (FTC) and the three main credit bureaus: TransUnion, Equifax, and Experian. It was designed to make it easier for you to obtain your credit reports. Make sure that you **download, print, or save each credit report** before moving on to the next one. Before printing, verify the number of pages of the report. Some reports can have more than 30 pages.

Get Started

Now it is time to establish a credit freeze on your credit reports. Your best defense against new account fraud is to establish a credit freeze with each of the five CRAs. Instructions are separated into five assignments, one for each credit reporting agency. Give yourself up to 30 minutes to complete each assignment. The amount of time is determined by if you prefer to establish the credit freeze by phone or online. I recommend that you complete these steps in a location where you have access to your financial records or your credit reports. You may need to refer to them when answering identity-verifying questions asked by the CRAs.

Before you establish a credit freeze, you should review your credit reports. As mentioned earlier, to request your credit reports from Experian, TransUnion, and Equifax

visit **AnnualCreditReport.com.**

To request your Innovis and NCTUE credit reports, visit their websites.

- Innovis.com
- NCTUE.com

If you do not want to establish a credit freeze, at a minimum, you should place a fraud alert on your credit reports by contacting the CRAs. Below are the phone numbers for each CRA.

- Innovis 1-800-540-2505
- NCTUE 1-866-349-3233

Call one of the below CRAs, and it will notify the other two on your behalf.

- Experian 1-888-397-3742
- Equifax 1-800-525-6285
- TransUnion 1-800-680-7289

Establish a Freeze with Equifax

Below are the step-by-step instructions to establish an Equifax credit freeze. Record all the information in the protection process worksheet or the workbook at the end of this book.

You can complete this step online or by calling their automated service at (800) 349-9960 to request a credit freeze. If you initiate a freeze using the automated phone service, Equifax will send you written confirmation by mail. I do not advise speaking with a human at Equifax. Their employees are trained to sell you their monitoring services.

Step One

- Create a MyEquifax account
- Visit **https://my.equifax.com/consumer-registration/UCSC/#/personal-info**
- Enter your information
- Confirm "I am not a Robot."
- Click "Continue"

Step Two

- Create your account
- Enter your email address; this will be your username
- Create a password
- Confirm your password
- Accept the "terms of use."
- Click "Continue"

Step Three

- Verify your identity by answering the questions
- Click "Continue"

Step Four

Once you have created your MyEquifax account, you can activate a credit freeze. The final step will provide you with a confirmation and your PIN. Print the confirmation page and record your PIN in the worksheet or workbook at the end of this book.

EQUIFAX WORKSHEET

To create, temporarily lift, or remove a credit freeze

Call (800) 349-9960 OR Visit MyEquifax

https://my.equifax.com/consumer-registration/UCSC/#/personal-info

MyEquifax Online Account

Created account on _____(date)

Username

Password

Credit Freeze PIN_____

Freeze created on _____(date)

_____

Password Reset Questions

Question One

Answer

_____

NOTES:

Establish a Freeze with Experian

Below are the step-by-step instructions to establish an Experian credit freeze. Record all the information in the protection process workbook.

You can complete this step online or by calling their automated line at (888) 397-3742 to request a credit freeze. If you choose to activate your credit freeze using the automated number, record your transaction ID number on the protection process worksheet. You will receive your confirmation letter and PIN by mail within ten business days. I do not advise speaking with a human at Experian. Their employees are trained to sell you their monitoring services.

Step One

- Visit **https://www.experian.com/freeze/center.html**
- Click on "Add a security freeze."

Step Two

- Select "Freeze my own credit file"

Step Three

- Enter your information
- "Would you like to select your own PIN?" Select "**No**" (Prevents you from having to think up a random PIN)
- Click "Submit"

Step Four

- Answer the identity verifying questions

Step Five

If answered correctly, you will arrive at the confirmation page. Print or download the page and record your PIN on your protection process worksheet and attach a copy of your confirmation page.

EXPERIAN WORKSHEET

To create, temporarily lift, or remove a credit freeze

Call (888) 397-3742 OR Visit Experian freeze center **https://www.experian.com/freeze/center.html**

Experian Credit Freeze

PIN _____

Created on _____

Transaction ID or Confirmation Number _____

The below section will be used if Experian permits online accounts in the future

Created account on_____(date)

Username

Password

_____

Password Reset Questions

Question One

Answer

Question Two

Answer

_____

NOTES:

Establish a Freeze with TransUnion

Below are the step-by-step instructions to establish a TransUnion credit freeze. Record all the information in the protection process workbook. You can complete this step online or by calling their automated line at (888) 909-8872 to request a credit freeze. If you choose to use the automated number, you will receive your confirmation letter and PIN by mail within ten business days. I do not advise speaking with a human at TransUnion. Their employees are trained to sell you their monitoring services.

- Visit **https://www.transunion.com/credit-freeze**
- Click on "Add Freeze"

Step One

- Enter your information
- Select "no" to opt-out of receiving promotional offers from TransUnion
- Click "Submit & Continue to 2"

Step Two

- Create a username
- Create a password
- Enter the password again
- Select a Secret Question
- Provide an answer for the Secret Question

Step Three

- Verify your identity by answering four multiple-choice questions.
- Select "Continue"

Step Four

- Create your PIN

Congratulations! Record your PIN on the protection process workbook and attach the confirmation page. Remember to log out at the top right side of the website.

TRANSUNION WORKSHEET

To create, temporarily lift, or remove a credit freeze

Call 888-909-8872 OR Visit TU freeze center **https://www.transunion.com/credit-freeze**

TU Freeze Center Online Account

Created account on _____(date)

Username

_____

Password

_____

Credit Freeze PIN

_____

Freeze Created on _____(date)

Password Reset Questions

Question One

_____

Answer

_____

Question Two

_____

Answer

_____

Question Three

_____

Answer

_____

NOTES:

Establish a Freeze with Innovis

Below are the step-by-step instructions to establish an Innovis credit freeze. Record all the information in the protection process workbook.

You can complete this step online or by calling their automated line at (800) 540-2505 to request a credit freeze. Innovis will send you written confirmation, including your PIN, by mail.

- Visit **https://www.innovis.com/personal/securityFreeze**
- Choose your preferred option. To establish a credit freeze online, select "Security Freeze Request Online"
- Select "Request a Security Freeze" in the Request Type section
- Enter your information
- Select "No, I am not a victim of identity theft."
- Enter your address
- Submit

If you entered the information correctly, you will see the confirmation page. Record the date on the protection process workbook. You will receive a confirmation letter, including your PIN, by mail within 7-10 business days. Record your PIN in your protection process workbook and attach the confirmation letter.

If you do not see the confirmation page, follow the instructions displayed on the website. It could be due to Innovis not having your information in their database. You could try to request a freeze by calling them at 1-800-540-2505.

INNOVIS WORKSHEET

To create, temporarily lift, or remove a credit freeze

Call (800) 540-2505 OR Visit INNOVIS **https://www.innovis.com/personal/securityFreeze**

INNOVIS credit freeze

PIN_____

Created on _____(date)

Transaction ID or Confirmation Number

_____

The below section will be used if INNOVIS permits online accounts in the future

Created account on_____(date)

Username

Password

_____

Password Reset Questions

Question One

Answer

Question Two

Answer

_____

NOTES:

Establish a Freeze with NCTUE

Below are the step-by-step instructions to establish an NCTUE credit freeze. Record all the information in the protection process workbook.

You can complete this step online or by calling their automated line at (866) 343-2821 to request a credit freeze. NCTUE will send you written confirmation by mail.

- Visit **https://www.nctue.com/Consumers**
- Select "click here" under the Security Freeze section
- Enter your information
- Click on "I am not a robot." and follow the instructions
- Accept the Terms of Service
- Click "Submit"

Step 2 of three

Select a Security Freeze Option you would like to request

- Place a Security Freeze
- Temporarily Lift a Freeze with a Date Range
- Permanently remove a Security Freeze

Note: You may be asked questions to validate your identity. Answer the questions and proceed.

Once you get to the confirmation page, you will need to print or download the information. When you open the PDF, it may appear to be a blank page. It is not; it is the cover page. Scroll down to page two, and you will see the confirmation document, including your PIN. Print the documents and record your PIN in the protection process worksheet.

NATIONAL CONSUMER TELECOM & UTILITIES EXCHANGE (NCTUE) WORKSHEET

To create, temporarily lift, or remove a credit freeze

Call (866) 343-2821 OR Visit NCTUE http://www.nctue.com/consumers

NCTUE Credit Freeze

PIN _____

Created on _____

Transaction ID or Confirmation Number_____

The below section will be used if NCTUE permits online accounts in the future

Created account on _____(date)

Username

_____

Password

_____

Password Reset Questions

Question One

_____

Answer

_____

Question Two

_____

Answer

_____

NOTES:

Opt-Out of Preapproved Credit Offers

Did you know that junk mail could lead to identity theft? Specifically, the credit offers that fill our mailboxes. Now you can opt-out of preapproved credit offers. When you register for Opt-Out Prescreen, you are notifying the credit bureaus that they are not permitted to disclose your information for unsolicited credit offers.

To opt-out, visit **www.OptOutPrescreen.com**. When you use the online system, your registration is active for five years. If you mail the confirmation page, it is permanent. To print the confirmation page, read the first paragraph and click to print the confirmation page. Sign the page and mail to the address provided.

Remember, if you are married, each of you should register. Registration is by SSN and not by households.

Get Started

- Visit **www.OptOutPrescreen.com**
- Select either online for five years or permanent by mail
- Enter the information requested
- Print the confirmation page
- Sign and mail the page to the address requested

OPT OUT OF PREAPPROVED CREDIT OFFERS WORKSHEET

Visit **www.OptOutPrescreen.com**

Registration is per person, not per household.

Five year _____ (ONLINE ONLY)

Date requested online _____

Permanent _____ (SUBMITTED FORM BY MAIL)

Date mailed form _____

NOTES:

Block Unwanted Solicitation Calls

Phone solicitations are annoying. It is getting harder and harder to distinguish between a legitimate phone solicitation and a scam. One way to stop phone solicitations is to register your phone numbers with the federal Do Not Call program.

To register your phone number or numbers, visit **www.DoNotCall.gov**. Follow the instructions and enter the requested information. You can register up to three phone numbers, mobile or landline. Registration requires a double-opt-in. First, you register online. Second, a confirmation is sent to you by email for each phone number. You must open each email and click on the link to confirm the registration. If you do not open and click the link in each email, the phone number will NOT be registered.

Once registered, it can take up to 60 days to become effective. You may still receive phone solicitations during this time. After the 60 days, phone solicitations should cease. However, the following types of calls permitted with this program:

- Political ad calls
- Donation calls
- Companies where you currently have a business relationship
- Companies where you previously had a business relationship

. Get Started

- Visit **www.DoNotCall.gov**
- Enter the requested information
- Check your email
- Open the email for each phone number
- Click on the link in the email to confirm the registration
- Can take up to 60 days before calls are blocked

BLOCK PHONE SOLICITATIONS WORKSHEET

Visit www.DoNotCall.gov

Date of registration _____

You can register up to three phone numbers.

Phone Number One _____

Confirmed by email on _____

Phone Number Two _____

Confirmed by email on _____

Phone Number Three _____

Confirmed by email on _____

NOTES:

ACCOUNT TAKEOVER

Think you are safe offline, think again

Data breaches notifications are becoming so common that people are starting to suffer from alert fatigue. It has become so bad that you might be thinking to yourself, "I should go off the grid." Okay, maybe that is a bit extreme. It is, however, enough to make you think twice about being online.

Common sense would tell you that being offline significantly reduces your chance of having your information exposed online. Unfortunately, common sense does not exist in the digital age. At least not in this situation. In the digital age, your information is online regardless of if you put it there or not. A simple online search of your name may reveal your home address and telephone number. Like it or not, you are online and will be there forever.

What happens if you choose to stop participating in the online world? That is where things get risky.

If you choose *to not* participate in the online world, then you run the risk of someone else assuming your identity online. If you do not establish your online presence, an imposter will do it on your behalf. Eventually, he will become so intertwined with your identity that your friends and family may believe he is you.

Online accounts

An even greater risk is the risk of an imposter establishing an online account with your bank, credit card company, or telephone carrier. Many companies permit you to set up an online account to access and manage your account. Unfortunately, if you choose not to set up an online account, many of the companies do not have a way to disable this feature. While they may say that it can be deactivated, a simple call to the company is all that is needed to activate the account.

How do scammers set up your online accounts? First, they obtain your sensitive information such as your name, address, date of birth, and social security number, information that can be purchased online for less than one dollar. Now that he has your information, the imposter calls the customer service number for the organization, pretends to be you, and answers the identity verifying questions with the information he purchased online. Once he has access to your account online, he can do anything, including, but not limited to, transferring funds, forwarding your telephone calls to his mobile phone, or requesting a companion credit card.

The Solution

Your best defense against account takeover is to establish your presence online. If you already have an online account in place, it will be harder for a scammer to set one up. He would need to request a password reset, which would often trigger an email to your notifying you of the request.

Refusing to participate in the online world does not protect you from becoming an identity theft victim. It only makes it easier for a scammer to assume your digital identity.

Fraud Alerts and Monitoring

Did you know that most financial institutions and credit card companies offer you free tools to help monitor for fraud? While they work to monitor your account for fraudulent transactions, they cannot do it alone. They need your help. Only you know which transactions are and are not yours.

After creating your online account, you can take advantage of online services. One of which may include account alerts. Here are a few types of alerts available:

- Account balance
- Transaction amount
- Card not present (credit card was not physically swiped, most likely used online)

Once activated, you will receive an alert by email or text message. Alerts can be used to help you monitor for fraudulent transactions. I use online alerts and login to my financial accounts twice a day, once in the morning and again in the evening. The earlier you detect and report fraudulent transactions, the faster and easier it will be to recover.

If you have questions or need assistance activating online alerts, contact your financial institution or credit card company.

Extra Security: Passwords

A password is often the first layer of security to prevent unauthorized access to an account. However, passwords do have limitations.

What Are Passwords

Passwords were intended to protect your account because you, and only you, know the password. In the past, requirements for passwords were minimal. Originally, passwords were comprised of four to six characters, typically letters and numbers. It was soon discovered that four-character password was easy to crack.

The Problem with Passwords

More than a decade ago, while attending a private investigator conference, I learned of a software program that anyone could purchase online that would crack passwords. Basically, you downloaded the program and directed it toward a website's login page. The program would run until it figured out the password. Today, bad guys have access to super computers and botnets that take less two-and-a-half hours to crack an eight-character password. Even if the password uses letters, numbers, and symbols.

The Solution: Stronger Passwords

Strong passwords are passwords with a minimum of twelve characters. I know what you are thinking, "I will just add a few 1's or !'s to my current password." Not so fast. Don't think of a password as a word, think of it as a phrase. Use a line from your favorite song, book, or movie. Use your favorite saying. For example, you could use *FloridaRocksSnowSucks*. Sorry, my Floridian is showing.

Just remember, longer passwords are stronger passwords. They should also be unique for your accounts. If you reused your password and it was exposed, bad guys could use it to gain access to all your online accounts. No password recycling!

I bet you are asking yourself "How the heck am I supposed to remember all these passwords?" You could use the old-school method of paper and pencil. Just make sure you keep the document in a secured location. No, that does not mean under your keyboard or mouse pad. A sticky note on your computer monitor is also a bad idea. Store it in a locked file cabinet or hide it somewhere no one will find it. Just don't forget where you hid it. I am good at hiding things so well that I cannot find them.

Another option is to use a password manager; either could be a computer program you install on your computer or an app for your device. Depending on the password manager you choose, your passwords are stored locally (on one device) or in the cloud (accessible from any device). If your passwords are stored in the cloud, make sure the password manager uses encryption-at-rest and encryption-in-transit. Encryption-at-rest protects your passwords on the password manager's server. Encryption-in-transit protects your passwords when you are storing or retrieving them.

I do not recommend storing passwords in a notes-type of app on your device, unless the app is password protected. I also do not recommend storing them on your computer in a document or spreadsheet. If you insist on using storing your passwords in a document, please do not name the document "My Passwords." You should also, at a minimum, encrypt the document to prevent unauthorized access.

Extra Security: Two-Factor-Authentication

Two-factor-authentication, known as 2FA, was intended to add an extra layer of protection to online accounts.

What is Two-Factor Authentication

Two-Factor Authentication, 2FA, is an extra layer of security to prevent someone from accessing your online accounts. 2FA requires two pieces of information to access the online account:

1. Something you know – your password
2. Something you have – access to your email or text messages.

Often, you can select your preferred method of receiving the code: text or email. After you enter your password, you are prompted to enter the code sent to you by either text message or email.

The Problem with 2FA

Just like with any anti-fraud prevention, the bad guys are always a few steps ahead. They have discovered ways to circumvent 2FA. One way is through SIM Swapping, mentioned in chapter two.

In your mobile phone is a SIM card. The SIM card is what makes your mobile phone send and receive calls and text messages and access the internet. Each SIM card has a serial or identifying number. The number is used to match your phone with your mobile service. SIM swapping occurs when a criminal, pretending to be you, contacts your mobile phone carrier and has your mobile

service transferred to the SIM card in his phone. ALL your text messages and calls are now going to the criminal's phone, through the SIM code. Most often, the only information required to validate an account holder's identity is a name, address, date of birth, and SSN. This information is available for purchase online for less than one dollar.

Now that the criminal has your mobile services assigned to the SIM card in his phone, he will visit the major financial institution and email account websites. Next, he will initiate a password reset. Often, these companies will send a verification code to the account owner via text message.

The difference is that the text message sent to your phone number will not show up on your phone. It will show up on the criminal's phone.

To minimize the risk of SIM swapping, contact your mobile phone carrier and ask about extra security, a PIN. Make sure that your PIN is nothing linked to you. DO NOT use your birthday, anniversary, year of birth, the numerical portion of your street address, your child's birthday, or the last four digits of your phone number or SSN. Have I guessed yours? Use random numbers. If not, a criminal can guess your PIN and SIM swap you.

The Solution: Choose Email

Until there is a viable solution to defend against SIM swapping, your best defense is to choose to receive the 2FA code by email. Emails do not automatically transfer to a SIM Card. Email accounts must be set up on a new phone.

It is crucial that the password for your email account is changed every year and that you use a strong password. A strong password has a minimum of twelve characters. Don't think of it as a password. Think of it as a passphrase. Use a line from your favorite movie, song, or book. Longer is stronger.

Extra Security: Security Questions

Security questions are another form of identity verification used by financial institutions and other organizations. The increase in fraud and identity theft has prompted these companies to implement additional security to distinguish you from an imposter. But do they work?

What Are Security Questions

Before we look at the effectiveness of security questions, first we need to understand how they work. Security questions are not to be confused with knowledge-based questions or answers. When asked

a knowledge-based question, your ability to answer it correctly authenticates your identity. With knowledge-based questions, the organization already knows the correct answer. *You were never asked to create an answer.* The organization is confirming information from a database that contains information about you, such as your credit history report. If you answer the question incorrectly, you will not be permitted to access the account or information which you were seeking.

Security questions, on the other hand, are questions to which the answer is the one that you provide. Any answer you provide becomes the true answer. To make it easier, let's look at an example. If asked, "What was your high school mascot?" Your answer could be "blue" or "chair" or any word or word you wish to use. This answer then becomes the correct answer from that point forward.

The Problem with Security Questions

Most people tend to answer security questions with real answers. Why? Because it is easier to remember, and it is the truth. If you choose to answer security questions with real answers, you run the risk of an imposter being able to answer them as well. Think about a few of the most common security questions.

- What was your high school mascot?

- What was the name of your middle school?

- What was your first car?

- What is your favorite movie?

A simple internet search could reveal most of these answers. Don't believe me? Have you ever participated in a social media poll, quiz, or game? These are the ones that typically start with "Let's get to know each other better." followed by a series of questions that appear to be innocent enough that you let your guard down and play along. Or perhaps, in your profile, you mention where you went to school as well as your hobbies and interests. All of these are designed to harvest your security question answers. A few years ago, a local celebrity posted, "This was my first car, what was yours?" on her social media page. Within an hour, there were nearly a hundred replies to the post from followers. All of them contained information about their first car: I contacted the organization where this person worked and suggested that they remove the post. The person inquired as to why. I explained that the post was a common security question. The person on the phone paused and said,

"That is the security question for my bank account." They agreed to remove the post. A good rule to follow when using social media: if you wouldn't post it on a billboard on the highway, do not post it online.

The Solution: The One-Off Method

Now that you know the risk of using real answers, you are probably thinking, "Great; now I have to remember fake answers along with all of my passwords and PINs." Don't panic. I have a simple solution. I call it a "one-off." Instead of answering the security questions based on your information, choose someone that you know to be your answer key. Then answer the security questions using the answers of the person you chose as your answer key. If asked, "What was your high school mascot?" you would not put your high school mascot. You would answer with your answer key person's high school mascot. Your answer key person could be a relative, best friend, or favorite movie character. The only person I do not recommend using is the person that has the same answers as you. That would defeat the purpose of using the one-off. By using the one-off method, you do not have to remember fake answers. The only thing you need to remember is the person that is your answer key.

Social Media Account Takeover and Cloning

Have you ever received a friend request online only to later discover it was not from your friend? IF so, you have observed cloning. Once someone has cloned your identity on social media, he will wait for your friends and family to find him, or he will send them a friend request. Once accepted, the scammer will then begin to communicate with your friends and family to either scam them or learn more about you. Search your name on social media websites. Have you been cloned?

You have options to protect yourself from cloning.

1. Establish your social media profile. Send friend requests to your friends and family. Then if your friends or family receive a second friend request, they will know it is an imposter. Just because you have established your profile, it does not mean that you need to upload additional information. You control how much or how little you choose to share.

2. Avoid it altogether, but make sure you tell your friends and family that you would never have a social media account. This way, if they receive a cloned friend request, they will know it is from an imposter. It does not affect people outside of your friends and family. The imposter may still be able to use the cloned account to become you online to others.

Get Started

- Activate your online accounts or contact the organization about adding extra security.
- Use monitoring tools and alerts
- Login to your account to monitor your transactions
- Answer security questions using the "one-off" method

CHILD IDENTITY THEFT

Children are a favorite target of identity thieves. By using a child's identity, a thief can typically go undetected for up to eighteen years. Most victims do not discover identity theft until they apply for college or attempt to obtain their first credit card. Both do not occur until the child is approaching or has approached his eighteenth birthday. What can you do to protect your children from becoming the next identity theft statistics?

Preventing all types of child identity theft is impossible. However, there are steps you can take to reduce the risk of credit-related identity theft greatly.

Credit Freeze

A credit freeze prevents any new creditors from ever seeing the credit report. If a potential creditor cannot see the credit report to determine credit worthiness, they will not open the account. A credit freeze is your best defense against new (credit) account fraud. However, you can only place a credit freeze on an established credit record. Minors typically do not have a credit record. Therefore, a credit freeze would not be possible. Or in other words, how can you freeze something that does not exist?

The 2018 amendment to the FCRA overcame this problem by permitting a credit record to be established without having to first apply for credit. A credit report is then created for your child, then frozen. If you are the parent or legal guardian of a child under 16, you can place a security freeze on their credit reports. You'll need to provide proof of your identity and theirs and proof that you are their parent or legal guardian. The request must be in writing.

Visit my website, **CarrieKerskie.com/ProtectYourIdentity** to download the forms to request a credit freeze for a minor or incapacitated adult.

If an identity thief were to use your child's SSN as part of a synthetic ID, the credit freeze might not stop it. A synthetic ID is when an identity is created using information from multiple people. It could be the SSN of a child, the name of another person, and a made-up date of birth. Due to how credit reporting agencies manage credit, a child could still become a victim. Credit reporting agencies do not cross-reference the information with the Social Security Administration.

Here are a few more tips to reduce the risk of child identity theft:

- Protect your child's social security number. Before providing your child's social security number, ask if it is necessary, and how it will be protected. Ask if you can use another identifier or the last four digits of the social security number.

- Paper and electronic records with your child's sensitive information should be kept in a secure location.

- Shred all documents that show your child's sensitive information before throwing them away.

- Talk to your children about identity theft. Discuss what information should and should not be shared on the internet and why.

Pay attention to warning signs of child identity theft. These include:

- Collection calls or bills for products or services not received

- A written notice from the IRS saying your child owes income taxes or that your child's social security number was used on another tax return

- Credit card offers or statements for your child

- An Explanation of Benefits statement from your health insurance carrier for an unknown charge or service.

- Data breach notification letter

- Your child is denied government benefits because the benefits are paid to another account

- Your child has a credit report before activating the record.

If you observe any of these warning signs, please do not disregard them as an error. You must take immediate action by contacting the involved organization and requesting additional information. If you should need assistance, contact us at **CarrieKerskie.com.** Let us use our experience and knowledge to help you through the process.

DECEASED PERSON IDENTITY THEFT

Ghosting is a term used to describe the identity theft of a deceased individual. When a loved one passes, most people assume that someone will notify the credit bureaus. While this may be true, it is often not done as swiftly as it should be to prevent ghosting. Here are a few steps to take when your loved one passes.

Obituary

People often use the obituary to celebrate their loved one's life. Unfortunately, criminals use them to obtain sensitive information used to commit identity theft. When drafting the obituary, it is best only to state the decedent's age, not their full date of birth. You should also refrain from listing the mother's maiden name, their home address, or other sensitive information. The same is true of surviving family members.

Death Certificate

Request at least twelve copies of the death certificate. The death certificate is the official document that is used to notify organizations of your loved one's passing.

Credit Bureaus

Send a copy of the death certified by mail, certified-return-receipt, to each credit bureau and ask that they label the account "closed: account holder is deceased" or place a deceased alert on the credit report. Doing so will prevent an identity thief from obtaining new credit accounts using your loved ones' identity. The three major credit bureaus are TransUnion, Experian, and Equifax. Instructions to report a death to Innovis and NCTUE may vary. Contact each one directly.

If you are the executor of the estate, you may also request a copy of the decedent's credit report. Reviewing the report will provide you with information on creditors to contact as well as any potential identity theft. The Identity Theft Resource Center has created a template letter to report a death to the credit bureaus. The template letter, form 1171-1, can be downloaded by visiting the **IDTheftCenter.org** website or my website, **CarrieKerskie.com/ProtectYourIdentity.**

Months later, recheck the credit reports. Credit accounts should say "closed," and the credit report labeled as "a deceased person." Any inquiries for new credit should be contacted immediately, as this could be a warning sign of identity theft.

Financial Accounts

Financial accounts include banks, credit cards, brokerage, loans, and mortgage accounts. Each one should receive a copy of the death certificate. Request that every account is labeled "closed/deceased." If it is a joint account, ask to remove the decedent's name from the account. Each financial institution should send you written verification that the account was closed or the decedent's name was removed.

Social Security Administration

Contact Social Security at 1-800-772-1213 to report the death. The funeral director may handle this step, but now is not the time to make assumptions. It is best to double-check and contact them yourself.

State Department of Motor Vehicles

Contact the Department of Motor Vehicles in the state where your loved one had a driver's license. Inquire about their procedures to report the death and cancel the driver's license.

IRS

Report the death to the IRS. Someone might tell you that this is not necessary, as the filing of the final tax return serves as a notification. However, the final tax return might not be filed immediately. It could take months before the final return is prepared and submitted. By contacting the IRS immediately, you reduce the risk of someone filing a fraudulent tax return.

Other Accounts

- Insurance Companies: auto, home, and life insurance.
- Professional License: contact the licensing organization
- Memberships/Subscriptions: such as fitness centers, utilities, online accounts, or the local newspaper.
- VA: if your loved one was a Veteran.

By taking these steps, you will significantly reduce the risk of someone ghosting your loved one.

EPILOGUE: LOOKING FORWARD

If you are reading this, that means that you finished this book. Congratulations! Now you can go back to the protection process section and begin protecting your identity. But, before you go, there is one more thing to consider. The steps outlined in this book are accurate as of the publication date. When it comes to identity theft, fraud, cyber threats, they are constantly changing. The bad guys always seem to be one step ahead of the rest of us. Tomorrow, there could be a new type of identity theft or a new method used to steal your identity that does not exist today.

Technology has not only made it easier for us, but it has also made it easier for criminals. The main difference is that criminals devote their time to discovering and implementing methods to get between you and your information and your assets. How are you expected to keep up with it all?

One way is to improve your digital hygiene. No, I am not referring to using your mobile phone in the bathroom. Digital hygiene describes one's habits when using technology. A person with poor digital hygiene clicks on everything, uses the same password for all online accounts, and has no interest in learning more about the technology he uses. A person with good digital hygiene is cautious before clicking on links in emails, uses strong and unique passwords for his online accounts, and takes the time to learn about the technology he uses. Developing good digital hygiene habits is another step in the prevention process. How can you improve your digital hygiene?

The first step is to visit my website **CarrieKerskie.com**. There you will find information on my blog, listen to my podcast "Frauducation," subscribe to my newsletter, and more. You can also follow me on Twitter, LinkedIn, and Facebook. Depending on when you read this book, there may be more social media options. On social media, follow me **@CarrieKerskie.**

One more thing, I have a favor to ask. Please tell me what you thought of this book. Was it helpful? Did you learn something new? I would love to hear from you. Send me an email at **ck@kerskie.com** or write a review. If this book helped you, tell your friends and family. You will help them protect their identity while helping me continue my mission. Now, go back through this book and start protecting your identity.

You can do it!

SECTION THREE: WORKBOOK

SECURITY ALERT

Using the Worksheets in This Book

The information you record in this book is PRIVATE and must be protected. Secure this book in a locked file cabinet or hide it. Just remember where you hid it. I have hidden things so well that I cannot find them. Oh, and do not accidentally donate this book or give it to a friend.

Downloading the Workbook

Another option is to track your progress in a workbook downloaded from my website. To download a PDF version of the workbook, visit **CarrieKerskie.com/ProtectYourIdentity**. Again, the information you record in the printed workbook is PRIVATE and must be protected. It is crucial that you store the workbook in a secure location.

A Note About Links and Contact Information

The links, phone numbers, and instructions were accurate as of the date of publication. The organizations referenced could change their web links, contact information, instructions at any time. It is unreasonable to hold me accountable for such information as it is out of my control. Depending on when you purchased this book or downloaded the workbook, if a link, phone number, or other information no longer works, contact the company referenced at their website or by phone.

EMPLOYMENT IDENTITY THEFT WORKSHEET

My E-Verify

To learn more about **E-Verify visit https://www.e-verify.gov/**

To create a My E-Verify account visit **https://myeverify.uscis.gov/**

Created My E-Verify account on _____(date)

Username

Password

Backup Code

Password Reset Questions

Question One

Answer

Question Two

Answer

Question Three

Answer

Question Four

Answer

Question Five

Answer

Self Check

Checked on _____(date)

Self Lock

SSN Locked on _____(date)

Expires on _____(one year)

Challenge Questions

Question One

Answer

Question Two

Answer

Question Three

Answer

___

To learn more about self-lock visit **https://www.uscis.gov/mye-verify/self-lock**

NOTES:

SOCIAL SECURITY IDENTITY THEFT WORKSHEET

MySSA

*Visit **www.ssa.gov** to create an account or block electronic access*

(check one) Created account_____ Blocked access_____

Created on _____(date)

Username _____

Password _____

Security Questions

Question One_____

Answer _____

Question Two_____

Answer _____

Enhanced security: _____Text _____Email _____Other

NOTES:

TAX RETURN IDENTITY THEFT WORKSHEET

Visit **https:/www.irs.gov** to create your online account

IRS Online Account

Created IRS online account on _____(date)

Username

Password

Site Phrase

Site Image Description

___

IRS IP PIN

To learn more about the IRS IP PIN and to request an IP PIN visit

https://www.irs.gov/identity-theft-fraud-scams/get-an-identity-protection-pin

Requested IP PIN on _____(date)

PIN _____ Tax Season _____

NOTES:

MAIL IDENTITY THEFT WORKSHEET

United States Postal Service

Visit **https://www.usps.com/** to create your online account

Online Account

Created on _____(date)

Username

_____

Password

_____

Security Questions

Question One

_____

Answer

_____

Question Two

_____

Answer

_____

Informed delivery activated _____Yes _____ No

Activated on _____(date)

NOTES:

NEW ACCOUNT FRAUD WORKSHEETS

EQUIFAX WORKSHEET

To create, temporarily lift, or remove a credit freeze

Call (800) 349-9960 OR Visit MyEquifax **https://my.equifax.com/consumer-registration/UCSC/#/personal-info**

MyEquifax Online Account

Created account on _____(date)

Username

Password

Credit Freeze PIN

Freeze Created on _____(date)

_____

Password Reset Questions

Question One

Answer

_____

NOTES:

EXPERIAN WORKSHEET

To create, temporarily lift, or remove a credit freeze

Call (888) 397-3742 OR Visit Experian freeze center **https://www.experian.com/freeze/center.html**

Experian Credit Freeze
PIN _____

Created on _____

Transaction ID or Confirmation Number

_____

The below section will be used if Experian permits online accounts in the future

Created account on _____(date)

Username

Password

_____

Password Reset Questions

Question One

Answer

Question Two

Answer

Question Three

Answer

_____

NOTES:

TRANSUNION WORKSHEET

To create, temporarily lift, or remove a credit freeze

Call 888-909-8872 OR Visit TU freeze center **https://www.transunion.com/credit-freeze**

TU Freeze Center Online Account

Created account on _____(date)

Username

_____

Password

_____

Credit Freeze PIN

_____

Freeze Created on _____(date)

Password Reset Questions

Question One

_____

Answer

_____

Question Two

_____

Answer

_____

Question Three

_____

Answer

_____

NOTES:

INNOVIS WORKSHEET

To create, temporarily lift, or remove a credit freeze

Call (800) 540-2505 OR Visit INNOVIS https://www.innovis.com/personal/securityFreeze

INNOVIS credit freeze

PIN_____

Created on _____(date)

Transaction ID or Confirmation Number

_____

The below section will be used if INNOVIS permits online accounts in the future

Created account on _____ (date)

Username

Password

_____

Password Reset Questions

Question One

Answer

Question Two

Answer

_____

NOTES:

NATIONAL CONSUMER TELECOM & UTILITIES EXCHANGE (NCTUE) WORKSHEET

To create, temporarily lift, or remove a credit freeze

Call (866) 343-2821 OR Visit NCTUE http://www.nctue.com/consumers

NCTUE Credit Freeze

PIN _____

Created on _____

Transaction ID or Confirmation Number: _____

The below section will be used if NCTUE permits online accounts in the future

Created account on _____(date)

Username

_____

Password

_____

Password Reset Questions

Question One

_____

Answer

_____

Question Two

_____

Answer

_____

Question Three

_____

Answer

_____

NOTES:

OPT OUT OF PREAPPROVED CREDIT OFFERS WORKSHEET

Visit **www.OptOutPrescreen.com**

Registration is per person, not per household.

Five year _____ (ONLINE ONLY)

Date requested online _____

Permanent _____ (SUBMITTED FORM BY MAIL)

Date mailed form _____

NOTES:

BLOCK PHONE SOLICITATIONS WORKSHEET

Visit www.DoNotCall.gov

Date of registration _____

You can register up to three phone numbers.

Phone Number One _____

Confirmed by email on _____

Phone Number Two _____

Confirmed by email on _____

Phone Number Three _____

Confirmed by email on _____
NOTES:

INDEX

2FA.....*See* Two-factor authentication

account takeover.....................13, 26, 74

AnnualCreditReport.com ..55, 56, 57, 58

Apps...12

Bluetooth 12, 19

Business identity theft 9

Caller ID spoofing..............................13

Child identity theft.............................80

CRAs.................................53, 54, 57, 58

Credit card blanks 26

Credit freeze34, 41, 52, 53, 57, 58, 59, 60, 61, 62, 63, 64, 65, 66, 67, 68, 80, 93, 94, 95, 96, 97

Credit lock 53

Credit monitoring.............30, 31, 55, 56

Credit reporting agencies ....*See* CRAs

Credit reports7, 28, 31, 34, 54, 55, 56, 57, 58, 80, 82

Credit-related identity theft.................31

Criminal identity theft.........................7

Dark web

Deep web 13

Data recovery 13

Deceased individual............................82

DoNotCall.gov........................71, 72, 99

Dumpster diving ....*See* Garbology

Employment identity theft 7, 36

Employment scam...............................14

Equifax31, 32, 40, 41, 45, 52, 54, 55, 56, 57, 58, 59, 82

E-Verify.............................36, 37, 38, 88

Experian31, 52, 54, 55, 57, 58, 61, 62, 82, 94

FACTA 55

Federal Trade Commission......30, 55, 57

Financial identity theft 5

Fraud alert.........................28, 51, 52, 58

Garbology 14

Gift cards 27

Government documents and benefits identity theft...6

Identity theft protection services..........30

Informed Delivery 48, 49

Innovis 52, 54, 58, 65, 82

IRS6, 7, 10, 12, 41, 44, 45, 46, 47, 81, 83, 91

Keyloggers 15

knowledge-based question 78

Mail theft 48

Malware 15

Man-in-the-middle (MITM) 16

Medical identity theft 8

MITM .... *See* Man-in-the-middle

Mobile pay 27

MySSA 40, 41, 42, 43, 90

NCTUE 52, 54, 58, 67, 68, 82, 97

New account fraud 1, 27, 51, 93

Novelty ID 7, 8, 27, 28, 48

One-off-method 75, 79

OptOutPrescreen.com 69, 70, 98

passwords 15, 75, 76, 79, 85

Phishing 16

Phone account 6, 27, 28

Phone solicitations . *See* DoNotCall.gov

Polls .... *See* surveys

Printable checks 29

Public records 17

Ransomware 18

Restoration services 31

Security questions 77, 78

Shimmer 19

SIM card 77

SIM swapping 76

Skimmers 19

Smishing 20

Social engineering 17

social media 21, 78, 79, 85, 102

Social Security Administration*See* MySSA

Spear phishing 20

Spyware 15

SSA*See* Social Security Administration

Surveys 20, 21

Tax return identity theft 44

TransUnion31, 52, 54, 55, 56, 57, 58, 63, 82

Trojan 15, 16, 25

Two-factor-authentication 76

Typosquatting 22, 23

United State Postal Service

   USPS 48, 49

USB 21, 22, 23, 24

Utility identity theft 6

Virus 15

Vishing 24

voicemail 24

Wardriving 24

Warning signs 9, 10, 11

Wi-Fi 14, 22

Carrie Kerskie is a highly sought-after national lecturer, author, and consultant on the topics of identity theft, fraud, and data privacy. She has presented at over 300 conferences, meetings, and corporate training events. Carrie is the President of Kerskie Group, an identity restoration firm, and CEO of Griffon Force, a leading identity theft, fraud, and cyber threat educational advisory firm serving consumers and small businesses.

Carrie is an identity theft victim advocate. For more than fifteen years, Carrie and her team have helped victims restore their identities. Carrie was the driving force behind strengthening Florida's identity theft laws and was lauded for her work with a Congressional Record from Congressman Mario Diaz Balart.

She is the author of the book, *Your Public Identity; Because Nothing is Private Anymore.* Carrie, a media favorite, was quoted in numerous publications, including Consumer Reports, Huffington Post, MarketWatch, Washington Post, KrebsOnSecurity.com, and TechRepublic.com. She appears regularly on various news programs on NBC, ABC, Fox, and NPR.

Connect with the author
- www.CarrieKerskie.com
- Subscribe to her podcast - Frauducation
- Follow her on social media @CarrieKerskie

Made in the USA
Monee, IL
24 August 2021

76412023R00063